LEARN TO SEW

LEARN
TO
SEW

....

CHRIS JEFFERYS

CRE🏠TIVE
ARTS & CRAFTS™

First published in 2005 by

CRE▲TIVE
ARTS & CRAFTS™

An imprint of Creative Homeowner®
Upper Saddle River, NJ
Creative Homeowner® is a registered trademark of Federal Marketing Corp.

Current printing (last digit) 10 9 8 7 6 5 4 3 2 1

Learn to Sew
Library of Congress card number: 2004113794
ISBN: 1-58011-243-9

Senior Editors: Clare Sayer, Steffanie Brown
Production: Hazel Kirkman
Design: Frances de Rees
Photographer: Shona Wood
Illustrations: Carrie Hill
Editorial Direction: Rosemary Wilkinson

Reproduction in Singapore
Printed and bound in Malaysia

CREATIVE HOMEOWNER
A division of Federal Marketing Corp.
24 Park Way
Upper Saddle River, NJ 07458
www.creativehomeowner.com

CONTENTS

	Introduction	6
	Basic Information	8
Technique	Getting Started	12
Project	Striped Pillow Covers	18
Technique	Hems	22
Project	Tie-Top Curtains	26
Project	Child's Apron	30
Technique	Curved Seams and Binding	34
Project	Clothespin Bag	36
Technique	Casings	40
Project	Drawstring Bag	42
Technique	Mitered Corners and Borders	44
Project	Tablecloth and Napkin	46
Project	Table Runner with Mitered Border	50
Technique	Fastenings	54
Project	Buttoned Pillow	59
Project	Zip-Up Bags	62
Technique	Piping, Gathers, and Pleats	66
Project	Chair-Seat Cover	70
Technique	Finishing Touches	74
Project	Pockets and Patches	76
Project	Calico Shopping Bag	80
Project	Wall Hanging with Pockets	84
Project	Silverware Roll	88
	Template	92
	Suppliers	93
	Index	95

Basic Information

Choosing the right fabric and good basic equipment will make it easier to develop your sewing skills, and will help produce successful projects. While most sewing equipment is relatively inexpensive, a sewing machine is a somewhat expensive investment and should be considered carefully.

A GOOD BASIC SEWING KIT

While there are many sewing aids that you will undoubtedly find useful as your skills progress, the items described here form a good basic kit. As a general rule it is always worthwhile buying the best-quality items you can afford, specially when it comes to scissors and pins.

- A pack of assorted needles
- A box of dressmaker's pins
- Dressmaker's scissors or shears
- Small, sharp scissors for snipping threads and fabrics
- A ruler and a right-angle set square for drawing and measuring straight lines
- A tape measure for measuring lengths
- An erasable fabric pen, a sharp pencil, or dressmaker's chalk
- A good-quality steam iron (to be used between each stage of assembly)
- An ironing board (keep it set up all the time to encourage good pressing habits)

SEWING MACHINES

There are many types of sewing machines on the market at a great range of prices, a fact that can be both bewildering and intimidating for a beginner. When thinking about which type of sewing machine to buy, the most important consideration is the types of stitches you will use most often for the sewing you intend to do. That said, a good basic machine selection includes a straight stitch, a zigzag stitch, a three-step or tricot zigzag stitch, a blind hemming stitch, and a button-hole stitch.

Straight stitch

The straight stitch is the basic machine stitch used for stitching seams. The size of the stitches can be lengthened or shortened, but a medium-length stitch is the one used for most types of sewing. The straight stitch can be lengthened to the longest length on the machine to make a gathering stitch. Straight stitching is worked in reverse at the beginning and end of a seam to fasten off the thread ends and prevent unravelling.

Zigzag stitch

The zigzag stitch is worked over raw edges in order to make them neater, and to prevent the fabric from fraying. The stitch length can be adjusted lengthwise to space the stitches further apart or closer together; it can also be adjusted widthwise to make the stitch wider or narrower. A medium stitch in both length and width is usually best for making the edges of a garment look neater. The zigzag stitch can also be adjusted so that the stitches are close together. Stitches made in this way, which are commonly known as satin stitches, form the basic stitch for buttonholes, and are also commonly used to stitch appliqué.

Three-step zigzag or tricot stitch

A variation on the zigzag stitch, the three-step zigzag or tricot stitch has three small stitches along each leg of the zigzag. This stitch can be adjusted in the same ways as the zigzag stitch, and is similarly used to make fabric edges look neater. On some fabrics, especially fine ones, use of a regular zigzag stitch will roll the edge of the fabric over, forming an

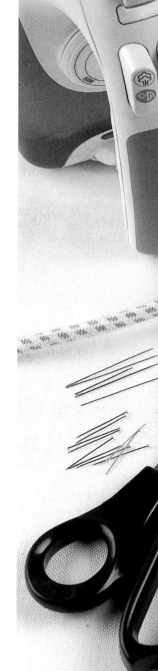

BELOW, counterclock-wise from left: steam iron, assorted needles and pins, dressmaker's shears, small scissors, tape measure, ruler, dressmaker's chalk, erasable fabric marker pen, right-angle set square, sewing machine.

unwanted ridge. Use of the three-step version avoids this result, giving a flatter finish. The three-step zigzag stitch is also useful for joining the ends of elasticized fabrics, and for stitching around the overlapped edges of a patch, such as on a sheet.

Blind hem stitch

This special hem stitch is worked on hems that are folded back on themselves. It stitches a few straight stitches along the hem fold,

then swings across in a single zigzag to catch the main fabric. This type of stitch can be an easier option to hand-stitching on long, straight hems, such as are necessary for curtains, but it is arguably too complicated to set up for short lengths.

Buttonhole stitch

Always try out the buttonhole stitch on any sewing machine you are contemplating purchasing. Many machines have automatic one-step buttonhole stitch-makers, which do not always make good buttonholes. While two-step or four-step buttonhole stitch-makers may seem complicated at first glance, they are actually quite easy to operate. A good buttonhole stitch-maker will have the stitches stitched forward, and those that are stitched backward will be the same distance apart. There will also be a clean channel along the center through which to cut.

CHOOSING FABRICS

The choice of fabric is a very important part of a successful project. As well as looking at the color and print of the fabric, always feel it as well, to see how it handles. Learn to distin-guish between fabrics with body, which will give shape to the item, and stiff fabrics, which may be treated with a finish that will wash out, leaving them limp and creased. On lightweight fabrics, hold up a length to check that it will gather and hang well, making sure it is a "fine" fabric as opposed to a flimsy one! Check to see what the fabric looks like when it is creased by scrunching up a corner and then releasing it. If in doubt, look and feel a fabric that has been used in a ready-made item to see how it suits its purpose.

Cotton

One of the most versatile and popular fabrics, cotton is ideal for many of the projects shown in this book. A natural fabric made from the hairs that cover the seed pod of the cotton plant, it is available in light to medium weights.

Cotton fabrics handle well, do not fray easily,

and respond well to pressing. There are many different types of cotton fabrics, as they vary according to their weave and finish. Some of the most popular cotton fabrics include gingham, chambray, poplin, denim, chintz, drill, ticking, cambric, and calico. Lighter-weight cottons include lawn and voile, both of which can be used for lightweight curtains.

Silk

Another beautiful natural fabric, silk is made from the pupae of the silkworm. Its inherent properties enable it to absorb dyes easily. This ability, together with its natural sheen, produces a wonderful range of deep, strong colors that cannot be achieved in other fabrics. Silk will crease a little more easily than cotton, but it presses well. Silk fabrics are prone to fraying and can be slippery to handle, so a beginner who wants to use them is advised to start with a very simple project. Silk dupion is a lightweight silk with a reasonably firm handle. It has an uneven slub weave that is part of its charm. Silk organza is very lightweight and sheer.

Wool

Made from sheep's wool, woolen fabric can be woven in many ways, creating a range of fabrics varying from fine wool challis to thick, hairy tweed. Woolen fabrics are generally warm, resist fraying, and handle well. These fabrics are used mainly for clothing.

Linen

Linen fabrics are made from the fibers of the flax plant, and are woven into light- to medium-weight fabrics. Most linens resist fraying and handle well, but are prone to creasing by virtue of the fabric's natural character. That said, the gorgeous sheen of linen is often thought to offset this drawback.

Man-made fabrics

Man-made fabrics are made from either chemicals or reformed cellulose, and include polyester, nylon, and rayon. Some of these fabrics are slippery and crease easily, while others, like polyester, are very crease-resistant. Man-made fibers are often mixed with natural fibers to produce a fabric possessing the best qualities of both fabrics. For example, polyester cotton voile has all the advantages of cotton together with the crease resistance of polyester.

CHOOSING THREADS

Threads are used for both hand- and machine-stitching. There are various types of threads on the market; choose according to fabric, permanence, and personal preference.

BELOW, clockwise from bottom right: gray and purple wools, white and blue linens, blue paisley and yellow polyester fabrics, blue checked cotton, green silk dupion, pink silk organza, yellow checked cotton, cotton flower print.

Cotton thread

Cotton thread is a fine, mercerized thread that is used for hand- and machine-stitching, usually on natural fabrics such as cotton, linen, and woolen fabrics.

Polyester thread

This is a popular, multipurpose type of thread that can be used on all types of fabrics. It is strong and comes in a wide range of colors. It is used for both hand- and machine-stitching.

Silk thread

Silk thread is a fine, yet strong thread that can be used for both hand- and machine stitching. It is used commonly on silk and wool fabrics, and for hand-stitched buttonholes on finer fabrics.

Bold thread

Sometimes called buttonhole twist, bold thread is a strong, thick thread that is used mainly for handstitching when extra strength is required. It is also used for handstitching buttonholes on heavier-weight garments.

CHOOSING NEEDLES AND PINS

Needles and pins will slip more easily through fabric if they are both fine and sharp. Choose a needle as fine as you can thread easily—a pack of assorted sewing needles is a good choice to start with. Thick needles or pins are difficult to push through fabric, and may leave unsightly holes on some fabrics.

Sewing machine needles

Most sewing machines come supplied with a packet of needles in various sizes, from 9 to 16 (the higher the number, the thicker the needle). A medium 11 or 14 works best for most fabrics, but the general rule is that the finer the fabric, the finer the required needle. If you break a needle while sewing, keep its flat side in the same position when replacing it so that the needle can catch the thread.

Pins

Pins are available with small metal heads or larger glass or pearl heads. The latter type can be easier to pick up and handle, but the choice is a personal preference. Extra-fine lace pins are available, but are really only needed for fine bridal and evening fabrics.

ABOVE, top row: packet of sewing machine needles; middle row, from left: polyester bold thread, cotton thread, polyester tacking thread, silk thread, polyester thread; bottom row, from left: pins with pearl heads, pins with small metal heads.

Getting Started

Before you start any sewing project, there are some essential techniques you will need to learn. This section takes you through the first stages, from pinning and basting to basic seams.

CUTTING YOUR FABRIC

Careful cutting out is the first step to success in any sewing project, however simple. All you need is a long ruler, a right-angle set square, a marker pen, and good dressmaking shears. (Bent-handled ones are easiest to use.)

Fabric is made in long lengths with finished edges called selvedges along the two side edges. Most fabrics are woven from two sets of threads: the warp threads that run along the length of the fabric parallel to the selvedges and the weft threads that run across the fabric between the selvedges. The grain of the fabric follows the line of one of these sets of threads. Ensure your fabric pieces are cut out accurately along the grain of the fabric.

To establish the widthwise grain, trim the edge along the line of a woven stripe or check, or pull out a thread across the width of the fabric and trim along the drawn line. On fabric where neither of these methods is suitable, the grain will need to be drawn at right angles to the selvedge, using a right-angle set square as a guide. Pieces are usually cut out with the warp threads running down the item and the weft threads running across, though at times this is reversed for special effect.

FINDING THE BIAS

The bias or crossway of the fabric runs diagonally across the fabric. To establish the bias, fold the fabric diagonally so the across grain edge is parallel to the lengthwise grain and selvedges. The diagonal fold is now on the bias (**A**). To make bias or crossway strips, cut along this fold. You can then cut strips to the required width along the cut edge.

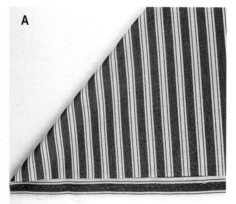

A

PINNING AND BASTING

Before stitching any two pieces of fabric, you will need to pin or baste them together. Basting is temporary stitching used to hold the fabric prior to it being machine- or hand-stitched. Use ordinary thread or speciality tacking thread—it is a good idea to use a contrast color so you can remove the tacking stitches easily.

1. Place the edges to be joined together with right sides together and the raw edges even. Pin the two layers together with the pins at right angles to the edge, or with pins along the seamline ⅝ in. in from the edge. Space the pins so they are about 2 in. apart, or further apart on firm fabrics.

2. If basting is required, begin and finish with one or two backstitches worked one on top of the other. Baste by stitching in and out through the layers of fabric, making stitches ⅜–⅝ in. long and in a line ⅝ in. from the raw edges (**B**).

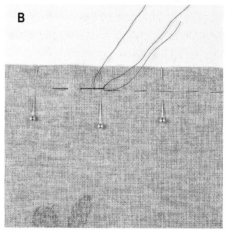

B

3. On the lengthwise pinning, remove the pins as they are reached. Remove the basting after the seam is stitched.

JOINING FABRICS

Most sewing projects involve stitching together two or more fabric pieces with seams, to make a larger piece of fabric or to make an item. This can either be done by machine or by hand. Machine-stitching is obviously much quicker and generally stronger, although sometimes, particularly on small areas, it is easier to stitch by hand.

Running stitch

This simple handstitch is useful on small areas, but is not very strong. Working from right to left, stitch along the seamline, taking the needle down through the two layers then back up again. Keep the stitches small and gather a few onto the needle before pulling the needle through (**C**). The smaller the stitches, the neater and stronger the seam.

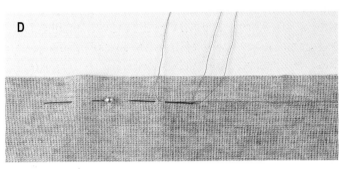

Backstitch

This is the strongest of the handstitches. Working along the seamline, take the needle down through the fabric and bring it back up about $\frac{1}{8}$ in. along (**D**). Take the needle back in at the end of the previous stitch and out again $\frac{1}{8}$ in. beyond where the thread emerges.

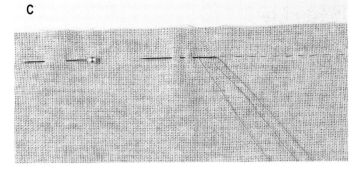

Ladder stitch

This neat handstitch is worked from the right side to match a pattern accurately, or to close an opening left in a seam.

1. Press the seam allowances to the wrong side along the edges to be joined. Butt the edges, matching the pattern if needed.

2. Take the needle along inside the fold of one edge for about $\frac{1}{8}$–$\frac{1}{4}$ in. Bring the needle out at the fold, take it directly across to the other fold edge, and stitch along inside that fold in the same way (**E**).

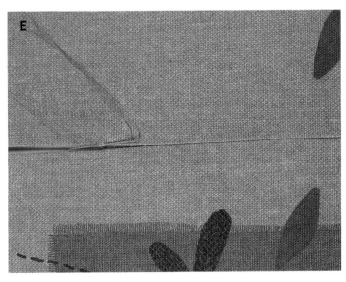

STARTING AND FINISHING

A neat, simple way to start and finish handstitching is with one or two backstitches. The stitches can be $\frac{1}{4}$ in. long. At other times it is best to make them as small as possible and position them where they are least noticeable. Make the stitch in the same way as the backstitched seam, but make a second stitch on top of the first.

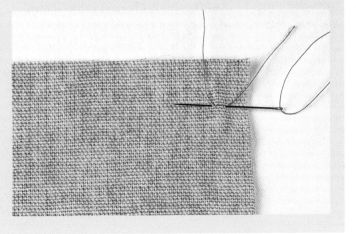

MACHINE-STITCHING

Machine-stitching is quick, accurate, and strong. It is well worth mastering the art of finishing ends securely and stitching accurately using the machine guidelines to keep the stitching straight and even.

Machine Back stitching

Back stitching at the start and finish of a piece of stitching will secure the thread ends, stop the seam from unraveling, and avoid the need to hand-finish the ends.

1. Begin stitching about $\frac{1}{2}$–$\frac{5}{8}$ in. in from the end of the seam, positioning the raw edges level with the $\frac{5}{8}$ in. guideline on the plate to the right of the needle.

2. Back stitch to the edge, then stitch forward along the seam, keeping the seam edges level with the guideline (**F**). Stitch to the ends, then back stitch for the same distance as you did at the beginning.

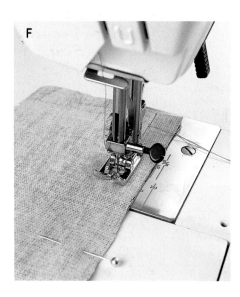

3. When the stitching is worked around in a circle, overlap the end of the stitching over the beginning by the same amount.

Stitching around corners

Stitch to the corner, stopping $\frac{5}{8}$ in. in. Make sure the needle is down—you may need to turn the wheel on your sewing machine towards you by hand. Lift the presser foot, turn the work, check that the new edge is level with the guideline, lower the presser foot, and continue along the next edge (**G**).

Stitching around curves

On smooth curves the fabric can be gently guided by hand. On tighter curves, as well as when guiding by hand, stop every few stitches with the needle down, lift the presser foot, turn the work slightly to realign, lower the foot, and continue (**H**). Try to stop and turn often when stitching a smooth curve, or you may end up with a series of short, straight lines.

MATCHING PATTERNED FABRICS

When you are joining fabric pieces together, it is often necessary to arrange the fabric so that patterns such as floral designs, checks, or stripes match together at the seam. This is particularly important when you are joining large pieces of fabric; for example, when joining two or more widths of fabrics for curtains. Patterned fabrics have a repeat—this is the distance between points where the same part of the design appears again. It is essential to know what this is when calculating fabric amounts, because you will need to allow extra fabric.

1. Press $\frac{5}{8}$ in. to the wrong side of the fabric along one edge. This is known as the seam allowance. Lap this edge over the other edge with the fabric facing right side up. Arrange the edges so the pattern matches exactly at the fold edge and pin the two layers together (**I**).

2. Knot the thread end, then, working from the right side, baste the two edges together by taking a stitch in and out of the flat fabric next to the fold, then slipping the needle into and along the fold edge for a short way. Keep the stitches about $\frac{3}{8}$ in. long.

3. Remove the pins and open the fold so the seam can be stitched from the wrong side.

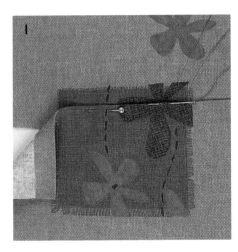

Matching stripes

1. To join stripes lengthwise along the seam, arrange the two edges with right sides facing, so the stripes match in the correct sequence along the edge of a stripe.

2. Pin along the edge of the stripe, checking that the pinning is accurate on both sides of the seam (**J**). Baste the seam, removing the pins as you reach them.

1. Stripes can also be matched in the same way as for a pattern. To match stripes at their short ends, arrange the fabric edges with

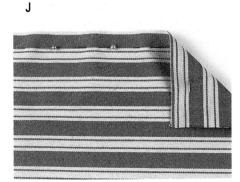

right sides together, raw edges even and stripes matching.

2. Pin along the edge of a stripe at right angles to the edges, checking that the pinning is accurate on both sides of the seam (**K**). Pin closely and baste over the pins. Machine-stitch, removing the pins as you reach them.

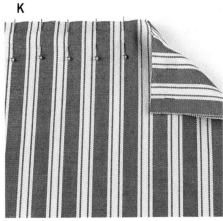

Matching seams

Place the two pieces of fabric together with right sides facing and raw edges even. Match the seams and pin at right angles to the edge, through the actual seam stitching (**L**). Check that the pinning is accurate on both sides. Pin, again at right angles to the edge, along the edges of the seam allowances. Baste over the pins and then machine-stitch, removing the pins you reach them.

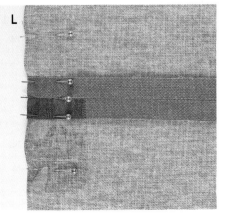

MACHINE-STITCHED SEAMS

Seams join pieces of fabric together and form the basic structure of all sewn items.

Plain seam

A plain seam is quick, neat, and long-lasting. Pin and baste the seam as required. Back stitch at each end and stitch the seam along the seamline, using the guides on the machine to keep the stitching evenly spaced in from the edge (**M**).

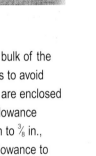
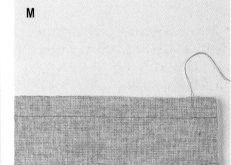

Layering

Layering a seam will reduce the bulk of the seam allowances on thick fabrics to avoid them forming a ridge when they are enclosed within an item. Trim the seam allowance nearest the right side of the item to $\frac{3}{8}$ in., then trim the remaining seam allowance to $\frac{1}{4}$ in. (**N**).

French seam

This is a neat, narrow seam for fine fabrics where the seam may show through.

1. Place the edges together with the raw edge even and the wrong sides facing. Stitch the seam $\frac{3}{8}$ in. in from the edges. Trim the seam allowances to a little less than $\frac{1}{4}$ in. and press them open (**O**).

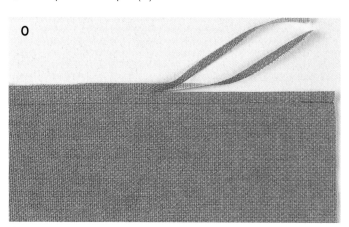

2. Fold the seam so the right sides are facing and press so the stitching is at the fold edge. Then machine-stitch $\frac{1}{4}$ in. from the fold edge so the raw edges are enclosed (**P**). Press the seam to one side.

Flat fell or shirt seam

This is a strong, flat seam used to join fabrics where an easy-to-launder seam is required.

1. Place the two edges together with wrong sides facing and raw edges even. Stitch $\frac{5}{8}$ in. in from the edge. Trim one seam allowance to $\frac{1}{4}$ in. (**Q**).

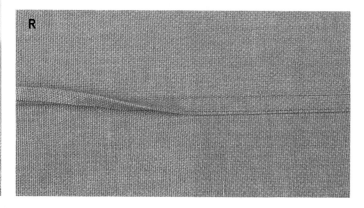

2. Open out the fabric and press the seam so the wider seam allowance lies on top of the trimmed one (**R**). Tuck the wider seam allowance under the trimmed edge and press. Machine-stitch the pressed fold down flat to the fabric. The finished seam will have two rows of machine stitching on the right side.

NEATENING SEAMS

When the edges of your seams are exposed on the wrong side of an item, they may need neatening to prevent the fabric from fraying. This can be done by pinking, zigzag stitching, or edgestitching.

Pinking

This quick method is useful on fabrics which do not fray easily, such as woolens. Special scissors called pinking shears are used to trim away just the very edge of the seam allowance, forming a zigzag shape (**S**).

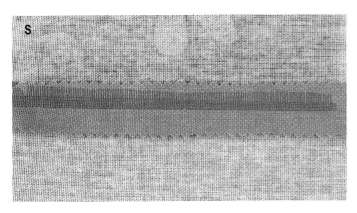

Zigzag stitching

This quick and durable machine method can be worked using an ordinary zigzag stitch, a three-step, or a picot stitch, which has three small stitches formed on each leg of the zigzag. Adjust the stitch to a medium length and medium width zigzag. If the seam is pressed open, zigzag stitch along the edge of each seam allowance separately (**T**). If the edges are pressed together to one side, zigzag stitch the two edges together.

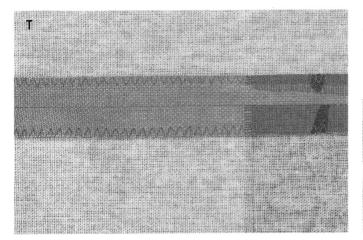

Edgestitching

This machine method is only used on pressed open seams. Fold and press $\frac{1}{8}$ in. to the wrong side along the edge of each seam allowance. Then, working from the right side, machine straight stitch along the fold through the seam allowance (**U**).

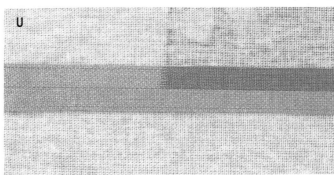

TRIMMING CORNERS

Corners need trimming carefully to prevent the seam allowances inside the corners from being too bulky when the corners are turned right-side out. On square corners, trim diagonally across the corner about $\frac{1}{8}$ in. outside the stitching at the point of the corner stitching (**V**). Loosely woven fabrics or ones that fray easily will need trimming a little further away from the stitching, while firm, fine fabrics may need trimming a little closer. If the corners are more sharply pointed, trim diagonally first, then trim away another wedge at each side of the corner. Turn corners right-side out by hand, then finish forming the point using a ruler or the closed end of dressmaking shears to gently push the point out. Avoid using anything sharp that could push through the corner.

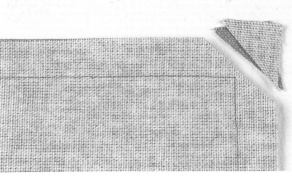

Striped Pillow Covers

Simple seamed fronts add smart designer detail to these easy cushion covers. Strips of silk fabric in a medley of tonal shades are stitched together to make a three-color cover. Striped fabric can also be used with great effect on a cover with diagonal seams. The cover backs are finished with straight hems on an overlapping flap, through which the pillow form is inserted.

Three-color pillow

MATERIALS
Pattern paper
Pencil and ruler
$\frac{5}{8}$ yd. silk dupion in three colors
Pillow form, 16 in. square

CUTTING OUT

1 Using the pattern paper, a pencil, and a ruler, draw out a pattern 17 in. square. Draw lines to divide the pattern into strips that are $9\frac{1}{4}$ in., $4\frac{1}{2}$ in., and $3\frac{3}{8}$ in. wide respectively. Cut along the lines, adding $\frac{5}{8}$ in. seam allowances to each cut edge.

2 Cut a piece of fabric for the back $26\frac{1}{2}$ in. wide by 17 in. long.

STITCHING

1 Stitch the wide and narrow strips to each side edge of the center strip with a plain seam (**diagram 1**). Press the seams open.

2 Cut the back piece of fabric in half along the 17 in. length. Press a $\frac{3}{8}$ in. then a $\frac{5}{8}$ in. hem to the wrong side along both cut edges and machine-stitch (**diagram 2**).

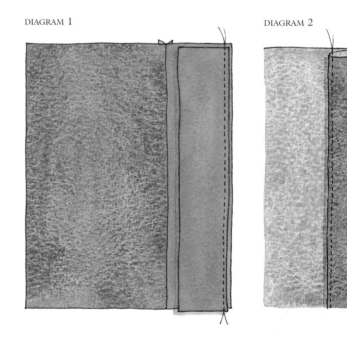

DIAGRAM 1

DIAGRAM 2

3 With right sides together, place the back pieces on the front so that the raw edges are even and the hemmed edges overlap. Pin the pieces to hold them together (**diagram 3**). Machine-stitch together around all four edges. Trim the corners and press the seams open as far as possible.

4 Turn the cover right-side out and press the seam at the edge. Insert the pillow form through the overlapping back edges.

DIAGRAM 3

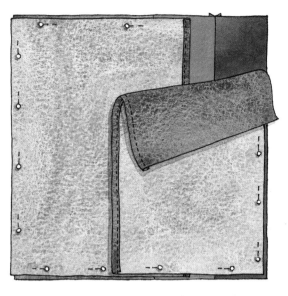

Diagonal Seam Pillow

MATERIALS
Pattern paper
Pencil and ruler
40 in. medium-weight, striped
decorator fabric
Pillow form, 16 in. square

CUTTING OUT
1 Using the pattern paper, a pencil, and a ruler, draw out a pattern 17 in. square. Draw lines diagonally across the square from corner to corner. Cut on the lines and add $5/8$ in. seam allowances to the cut edges on one piece to use as the pattern.

2 Cut out four triangular pieces of fabric, taking care to keep the long edge along the stripe or straight grain of the fabric and to match the stripe accurately on the shorter edges. This is easiest to do if you leave the first piece pinned to the pattern and use that to match the stripes on the next piece. Cut a piece of fabric for the back that is $26\frac{1}{2}$ in. wide by 17 in. deep.

STITCHING
1 Stitch two triangles together along one of the shorter edges, matching the stripes accurately. Press the seam open. Stitch the other two triangles together in the same way.

2 Place the two large triangles together with the center seam and stripes matching. Stitch together along the remaining diagonal seam and press the seam open (**diagram 1**). Make the cushion back and complete the cover in the same way as the three-color pillow.

DIAGRAM 1

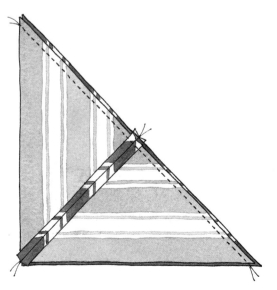

NOTE
For pillow covers that are larger or smaller than those in this project, measure the depth and width of the pad and add on 1¼ in. to each measurement for the pillow front. Cut the pillow back to the same depth as the pillow front. To allow for overlap, add 6 in. to the front width on pillows up to 13¾ in. squared, and 8 in. on larger pillows.

Hems

Hems are made to finish off a fabric edge neatly. A hem can be single, where just one layer of fabric is folded to the wrong side, or it can be double, where two layers are folded over. Single hems are used mostly on clothing; double hems are commonly used on soft furnishings.

BASIC HEMS

On a basic hem, just one layer of fabric is folded to the wrong side. Adjust the setting on your sewing machine to a medium-width and -length zigzag stitch and machine-stitch along the raw edge to prevent it from fraying. If the hem is to be covered by a lining, it can be left unneatened. Fold the hem depth to the wrong side and press. Pin and stitch the hem in place by hand or machine (**A**).

The most common type of hem has a small amount of fabric turned to the wrong side, and then the hem depth is folded and pressed again. To hem in this way, first press $\frac{3}{8}$–$\frac{5}{8}$ in. to the wrong side, then press the hem depth to the wrong side. Pin and stitch in place by hand or machine (**B**). If machine-stitching a single hem, stitch along just below the neatening, or stitch $\frac{1}{4}$ in. in from the edge.

DOUBLE HEM

This type of hem is used on very sheer fabrics to conceal the inner layer of the hem. First press the hem depth to the wrong side, then press the same amount again (**C**). Pin and stitch in place near the top fold. Double hems are usually machine-stitched.

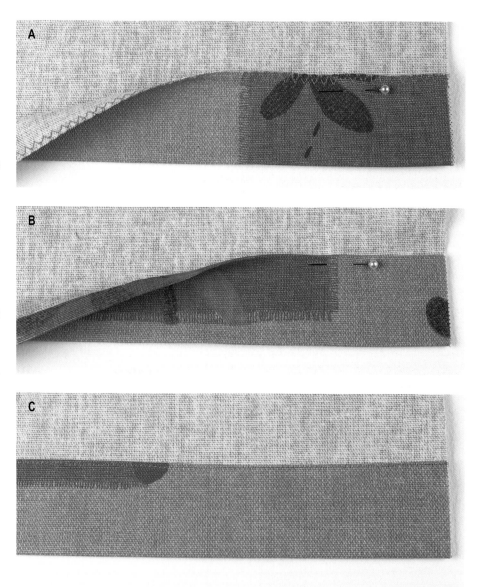

Shortening Trouser Cuffs

First establish the amount the trouser needs to be shortened, then measure and note the depth of the cuff. Unpick and fold down the outer part of the cuff. Measure and note the total depth of the cuff hem on the inside from the fold to the stitched edge. Unpick the cuff stitching, open it out, and press it flat. Measure, mark, and trim away the amount the leg is to be shortened. Press a new cuff hem to the wrong side to the same measurement as before, then stitch in place. Fold the depth of the cuff to the right side and then press. Stitch right through the seam line at both the inner and outer leg seams to hold the cuff in place.

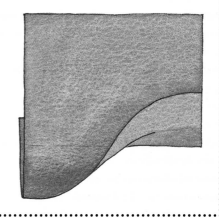

HEMSTITCHED HEM

This neat, handstitched finish can be used to stitch both single and double hems. Begin with back stitches near the fold of the hem, then stitch across to pick up just a thread of fabric above the hem (**D**). Stitch along diagonally back again through the hem. Repeat, taking care not to pull too tight.

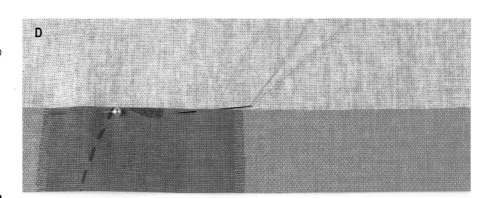

HERRINGBONE STITCH HEM

This handstitched hem is used to stitch single hems, usually on thick, nonfray fabric such as flannel or fleece. The stitching both neatens and stitches the edge so that there is no need to zigzag stitch the edge.

Working from left to right, begin with backstitches. Bring the needle through the hem, take it diagonally up to the right, and take a stitch through above the hem from right to left. Bring the needle diagonally down to the right and take a stitch through the hem, again from right to left (**E**). Repeat, taking care not to pull too tight.

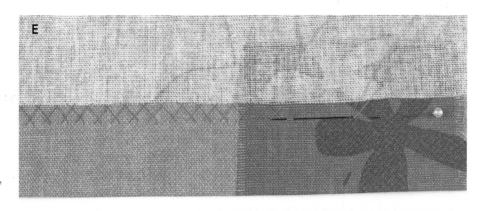

MACHINE-ROLLED HEM

This neat hem is easy to make once you get started, but the beginning can be a little messy, so it's worth allowing extra fabric to discard. Most machines come with a roll-hem foot that has a small metal scroll at the front that rolls and forms the hem prior to stitching.

1. Attach the roll-hem foot to the machine. At the hem's start, fold and press a double $\frac{1}{8}$ in. hem to the wrong side for 3 in.

2. Lower the foot onto the hem and stitch a few stitches while holding the bobbin threads at the back. Lower the needle and raise the presser foot. Unfold the pressed hem and guide it onto the scroll. Lower the foot and begin stitching (**F**), lifting the fabric edge and guiding it onto the scroll as you go.

F

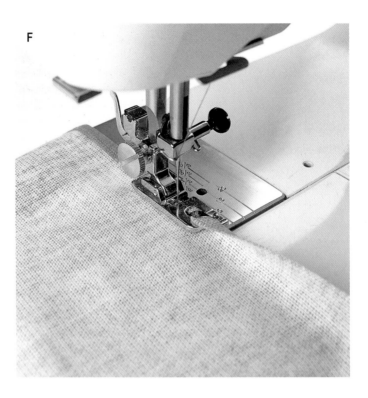

Hem Alterations

SHORTENING

When shortening a garment, mark the new hem level with pins and measure the amount by which you intend to shorten the garment. Unpick the existing hem using small scissors or a seam ripper, cut the thread, then open the hem out and press it flat. Measure the amount to be shortened in from the edge and mark it at intervals all around with an eraseable fabric pen. Trim away the fabric along the marked line so the hem allowance left is the same as the first hem. Refold the hem and stitch in place.

LENGTHENING

Unpick the existing hem using small scissors or a seam ripper, cut the thread, then open the hem out and press it flat. Refold the new, shorter hem to the wrong side and stitch in place. If the original hem line is worn or faded, stitch a narrow braid or ribbon over it. If a single row looks odd, add another row to make it into a decorative feature. On children's clothes, where the garment may soon need lengthening again, allow twice the hem amount and fold a double hem to allow fabric for lengthening later.

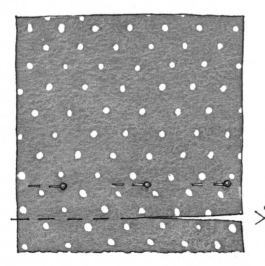

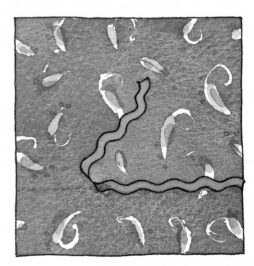

CURVED HEM

On curved hems the extra fullness can be eased in by one of two methods.

1. On a gentle curve, such as around a circular tablecloth, machine-stitch around the fold of the hem ⅝ in. in from the edge.

2. Using the point of an iron, press the hem over to the wrong side, rolling it over to form a smooth curve. Tuck under the inner edge of the hem to make a ⅜ in. hem, then pin and machine-stitch in place (**G**).

1. On tighter curves, stitch around the opened out inner fold of the hem with a gathering stitch. Pull up the thread to ease the fullness (**H**). Arrange the fullness evenly, then pin, tack, and machine-stitch in place.

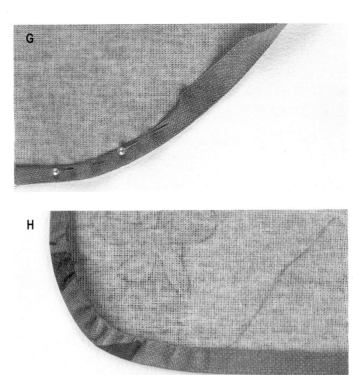

LENGTHENING WITH BIAS BINDING

On items being lengthened as far as possible, the edge can be finished with bias binding. Unpick and unfold the hem and press it flat. Unfold one edge of the binding and place it, right sides facing, to the hem edge so that the raw edges are even. Stitch in place along the crease of the binding (**A**), then fold the binding to the wrong side so that it forms the hem (**B**). Stitch in place.

BINDING A HEM

This method uses bias binding to finish a lengthened hem, but in this method the binding shows as a narrow border along the edge. If you cannot get a good match in the binding, choose a contrasting color. If the original hemline shows, a strip of folded binding could be stitched over the line to hide it (**A**). Unpick and unfold the hem, then press it flat. Unfold one edge of the binding and place it, right sides facing, to the hem edge so that the raw edges are even (**B**). Stitch in place along the crease of the binding, then fold just the edge of the binding over to the wrong side. Handstitch to the back of the first row of stitching.

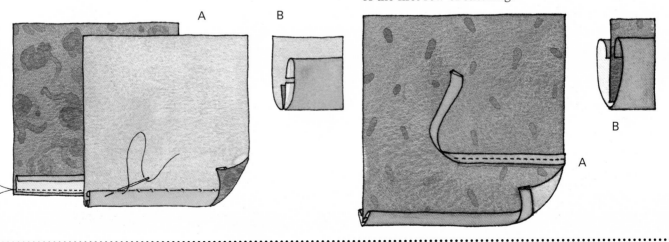

Tie-Top Curtains

Simple but effective, tie-top curtains are some of the easiest window treatments to make. For this project we have chosen satin ribbon for the ties, which are inserted neatly between each curtain and the facing strip that finishes the top edges of the curtains.

MATERIALS

Fabric of your choice
Ribbon, ⅝ in. wide, 16 in.
per tie

CUTTING OUT

1 Cut the fabric to the required length plus 4¼ in. by the required width, plus 1½ in. for hems, plus a fullness allowance. See below. Cut a separate 2¾-in. deep facing strip the same width as the curtains.

Fabrics and Fullness

Lightweight voiles and lawns are ideal for floaty tie-top curtains, though linens and cottons can also work well if you require a denser window covering.

The amount of fullness to add when making curtains is really a matter of personal preference. You could make your curtains flat, so they just cover the window area when closed, but they usually look better with a little fullness. Add about 8 in. per yard for a gentle fullness, or up to half the width again for a more gathered look. You could even allow twice the window width for a very opulent look. Try holding your fabric up and gathering it in your hands to determine how much fullness you prefer.

STITCHING

1 Press ⅜ in. then another ⅜ in. to the wrong side along the edges of each curtain to make a double hem. Machine-stitch in place.

2 Cut a 15¾ in. length of ribbon for each tie and press the ties in half. Mark the positions for the ties on the right side of the curtains, one at the edge of each curtain, then space the others evenly between about 6 in apart. Pin and baste the ties in place so that they hang downward and the fold is even with the top edge (**diagram 1**).

DIAGRAM 1

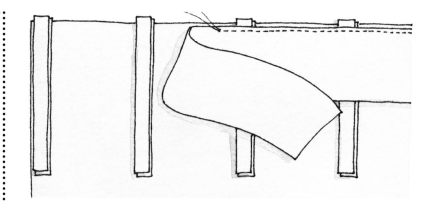

3 With right sides facing and the top raw edges even, place the facing over the ties, allowing it to hang over each end. Stitch the facing in place ⅜ in. down from the top edges of the curtains.

4 Trim the side edges of the facing ⅜ in. outside each curtain. Press the facing away from the curtains and press ⅜ in. to the wrong side around the remaining raw edges. Press the facing over to the wrong side of each curtain and machine-stitch in place along the side and lower edges (**diagram 2**). Then, if desired, machine-stitch along the top edge on the right side.

5 Press 2 in. and then another 2 in. to the wrong side across the lower edge of each curtain and machine-stitch in place.

DIAGRAM 2

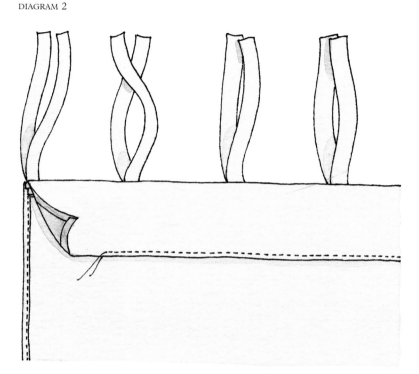

Give curtains that are too short for a new window a new lease on life with elegant border panels at the bottom and inside edges of the curtains. Broad panels stitched across the base add the required length, and the narrow vertical borders tie the new fabric in with the rest of the curtain. To join the old fabric with the new, unpick the curtain hems and trim the hem away along the hem fold line. Cut the new border twice the required depth, plus seam allowances. Stitch the border to the right side of the curtains, then fold half the depth to the wrong side and handstitch in place on the inside (**A**). Stitch the narrow border to the lead edges of the curtains in the same way.

A

Child's Apron

This useful child's apron has curved hems and a pocket. The straps for the waist ties and head loop have been made from the same fabric as the apron itself, but tape or ribbon could be also be used. The dimensions of this apron make it suitable for a child aged 4–7.

MATERIALS
Pattern paper
Pencil and ruler
40 in. cotton fabric

2 Draw out a pocket pattern 9 in. wide by 6 in. deep with a curved lower edge. Fold the patterns in half and cut out to ensure that both halves are symmetrical. Cut out the apron and pocket. Cut three straps 21 in. by $2\frac{1}{4}$ in. (if using fabric).

CUTTING OUT

1 Draw a line $7\frac{1}{2}$ in. long across for the top edge of the apron, then draw a line $23\frac{1}{2}$ in. down the center to mark the length (**diagram 1**). Mark $8\frac{1}{4}$ in. down from the top on the center line, then measure $8\frac{3}{4}$ in. out from either side of the mark to mark the side edges. Draw in the side and lower edges, joining them with curves at the lower corners. Then draw curved lines to join the top corners to the side edges to form the apron shape.

DIAGRAM 1

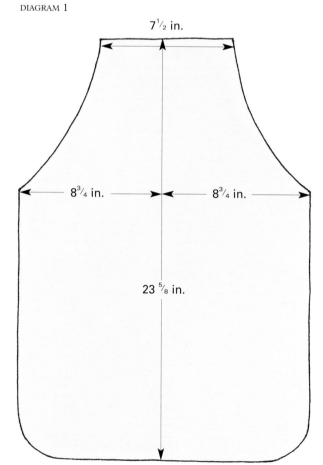

7$\frac{1}{2}$ in.

8$\frac{3}{4}$ in.   8$\frac{3}{4}$ in.

23 $\frac{5}{8}$ in.

STITCHING

1 Press ⅜ in., then another ⅜ in. to the wrong side on the curved side edges on the bib of the apron and machine-stitch in place.

2 Sew a gathering stitch around the lower corners ⅜ in. in from the edge. Press double ⅜ in. hems to the wrong side around the side and lower edges, pulling up the gathering stitching to ease the fullness evenly. Machine-stitch in place.

3 Stitch a row of machine-stitching around ⅝ in. in from the curved edge of the pocket. Using the stitching as a guide, press the seam allowance over to the wrong side so that the stitching just rolls over onto the wrong side.

4 Press ⅜ in., then ¾ in. hems to the wrong side across the top of the apron and the top of the pocket, then machine-stitch in place.

5 Press the pocket in half to mark its center. Place the pocket to the apron with its top edge 9 in. down from the top of the apron. Machine-stitch in place around the curved edges and down the center, following the crease as a guide.

6 Press ⅜ in. to the wrong side around all edges of the straps, then press the straps in half lengthwise and stitch along the length and across the ends. Underlap the ends of one strap under the hem at each side of the apron and stitch in place with a square of stitching. Stitch the other two straps to the top of the side edges in the same way (**diagram 2**).

DIAGRAM 2

NOTE

Aprons can suffer a great deal of wear and tear. To repair an L-shaped tear, cut a piece of matching or toning fabric about $^3/_8$ in. bigger all around than the tear. Place the fabric behind the tear and baste around the outer edge. Stitch in place with a close three-step zigzag stitch worked along the tear. On a larger tear, machine-stitch first forward, then in reverse, back and forth across the tear to form a close zigzag formation. When complete, trim the excess patch from the wrong side.

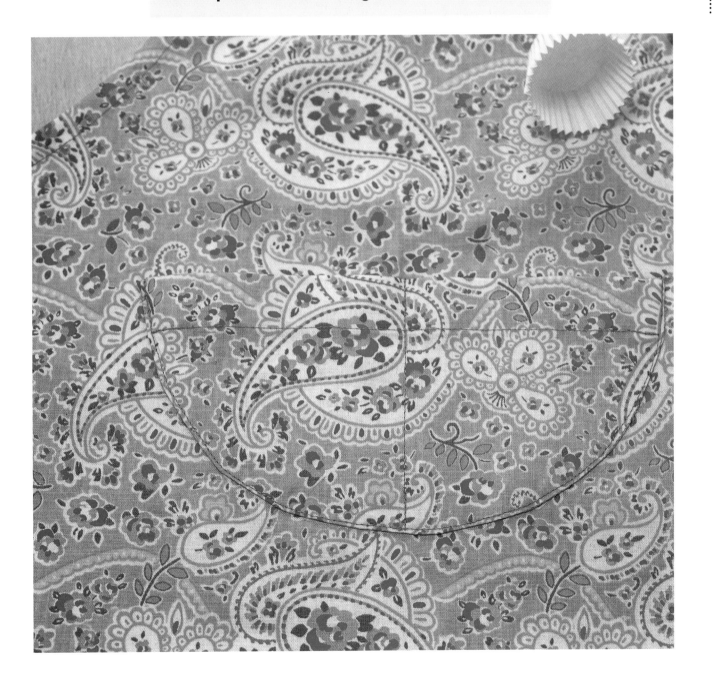

Curved Seams and Binding

Sometimes a project demands the fabric edge needs more than a simple straight seam to finish. Curved seams are stitched in the same way as plain straight seams but they need trimming and snipping after the seam is stitched. Binding is a neat and decorative way to finish a fabric edge.

CURVED SEAMS

Most curved seams will ease into shape more smoothly, particularly on small items, if the seam allowances are first trimmed to about half of their original width. The trimmed seam then needs to be snipped or notched.

Snipping into seams

When snipping into concave curves, such as the inside of a circle, snip into the seam allowance so it can expand when it is turned right-side out (**A**). On convex curves, such as the outside of a circle, small wedge-shaped notches should be cut out. The tighter the curve, the closer together the notches and the snips should be.

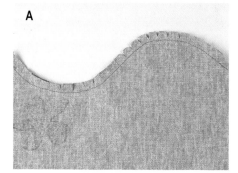

A

Scallops

Scalloped edges are often finished with a facing. This is a separate piece of fabric cut to the scalloped shape, but a bit deeper than the scallops. Stitch the facing to the scalloped edge with curved seams, then trim and notch the seam allowances as before. Also snip into the seam allowance at the top point between each scallop to just a couple of threads outside the stitching. Turn the scalloped edge right-side out and press the seam at the edge (**B**).

B

Topstitching

Topstitching is decorative stitching that is worked on the right side of the fabric, usually to outline an edge (**C**). It also often serves a functional purpose by creating a firmer edge or keeping a facing in place on the inside.

Topstitching can be worked near the edge of a fabric or a little way in. To keep the stitching even, use the guides on your sewing machine to keep the edge being topstitched level with the inner or outer edge of the presser foot so the stitching remains the same distance away throughout.

When you are topstitching a curved edge, work around the curve, stopping with the needle down every few stitches and turning the fabric slightly in the same way as you would when stitching a curved seam.

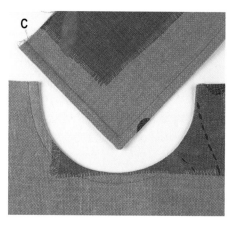

C

BINDING

Binding gives a neat finish to a fabric edge. The binding can be plain, to make a smart outline, or it can be checked or patterned to make a pretty edging. Bias binding can be purchased readymade, or it can be made from bias strips. Readymade bias binding is available in various widths—the finished binding will be half the width of the purchased binding.

Making bias binding

To make your own bias binding, cut long strips of fabric four times the required finished width diagonally across the fabric. This is called cutting on the bias. Then press both long edges in so that they almost meet at the center (**D**).

D

Joining bias strips

This neat method is used when it is necessary to join fabric cut bias strips to make up the length required.

1. Open out the binding folds. If required, trim the two ends on the straight grain. Place the two ends together with right sides together, straight ends even, and the foldlines intersecting ¼ in. in. Pin to hold.

2. Stitch the two ends together, taking a ¼ in. seam (**E**). Open out the binding and press the seam open.

3. Trim off the corners of the seam level with the edge of the binding and re-press the binding folds.

E

Binding an edge

1. Unfold one edge of the binding and place the raw edge even with the fabric edge on the right side of the fabric. Machine-stitch in place along the fold (**F**).

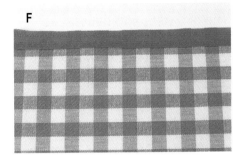

F

2. Fold the other edge of the binding over to the wrong side (so its edge is even with the machine-stitching) and stitch in place by hand (**G**).

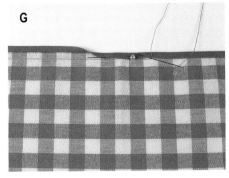

G

Joining ends

There are two ways of joining the ends of two binding strips. The first is to join the ends with a diagonal seam before the stitching is complete. An alternative, easier method is to overlap the finishing end over the starting end, tuck the raw end under, then complete the stitching (**H**).

H

Binding an edge: machine method

First unfold one edge of the binding and place the raw edge even with the fabric edge on the wrong side of the fabric. Machine-stitch in place along the fold. Fold the other edge of the binding over to the right side so its edge just covers the previous stitching and machine-stitch in place (**I**).

I

Binding an edge: sandwich method

Before stitching, fold and press the binding in half lengthwise so the upper half, which will be on the right side, is slightly narrower than the lower half. Sandwich the fabric into the binding and machine-stitch in place from the left side (**J**).

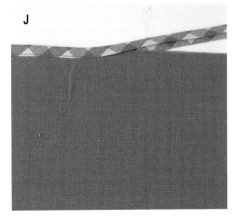

J

learn to sew

Clothespin Bag

**This handy bag, ideal for clothespins, has
a rounded opening at the front that can
be finished with either a simple facing or
smart binding. A wooden coat hanger, slipped
inside the top edges, suspends the bag from a
door hook or clothesline.**

MATERIALS
Wooden coat hanger
Pattern paper
Pencil and ruler
40 in. furnishing fabric

DIAGRAM 1

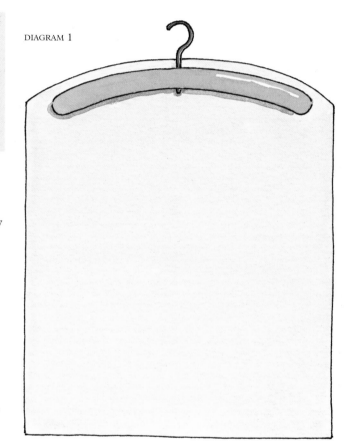

CUTTING OUT
1 Lay the coat hanger on the paper and draw
around its top edge and ends, then mark the
center. Add on ⅝ in. above the line, ¾ in. at
each side edge and draw in the base edge
19¾ in. down (**diagram 1**). Cut out two
fabric pieces to this pattern.

2 Draw a circular central opening about
11 in. from the top edge of the pattern. It
should be about 7½ in. wide. Draw a 1½ in.
facing around the opening. Cut out the opening for the front of the bag from one piece of
fabric. Trace off the facing pattern and cut
this out from the fabric.

STITCHING

1 Zigzag stitch around the outer edge of the facing to neaten. Place the facing to the opening with right sides together, and stitch in place around the opening, taking a $\frac{3}{8}$ in. seam allowance. Snip and notch the seam allowances around the curves and press the facing to the wrong side. Topstitch around the facing $\frac{3}{8}$ in. in from the edge.

2 Place the front piece to the back piece with right sides facing and outer edges level. Stitch together around the outer edges (**diagram 2**). Notch the seam at the curves and trim the corners. Turn the bag right-side out and press the seam to the edge. Slip the coat hanger inside the top edge to hang the clothespin bag.

DIAGRAM 2

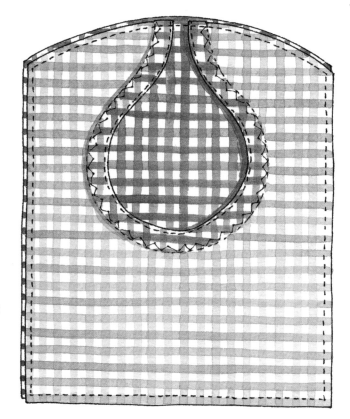

Bound Edge Alternative

An alternative to facing the opening, bias binding gives a neat contrast outline around the opening. As bias binding is always cut on the bias or crossways grain of the fabric, it should mold easily to sit smoothly around the curves. The binding shown here was first machine-stitched to the right side. The other edge was then folded over to the wrong side and hand-stitched in place using the method shown on page 35.

Casings

Casings form channels, usually at the top of a bag or the waist of a garment, through which cord, ribbon, or elastic is threaded to draw in the garment. Casings can also be made at the top of curtains to thread a pole or rod through. The casing can be sewn at the edge of the fabric, or it can be positioned just in from the edge, so that a frill forms above when it is drawn up. A casing can also be cut from a separate strip of fabric.

FOLDOVER CASINGS

This simple casing provides a channel to thread through cord or elastic. It is useful for making simple drawstring bags and waistbands.

1. First press ⅜ in. to the wrong side, then press the depth of the casing to the wrong side. Pin in place (**A**).

2. Machine-stitch in place along the lower edge (**B**). You can also stitch a second row of machine-stitching around the top of the casing to give it a neat finish.

A

B

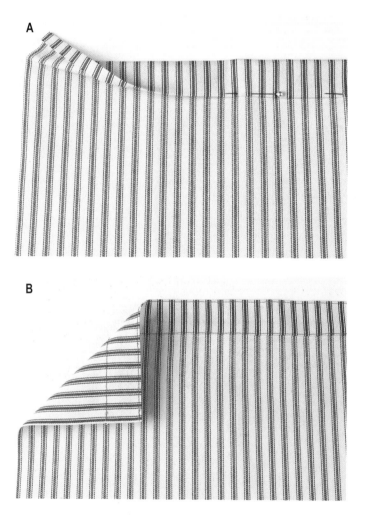

SELF-FRILL CASINGS

This type of casing is similar to the foldover casing, but here the channels are stitched in from the edge so that a frill of fabric stands up above the casing.

1. First press $\frac{3}{8}$ in. to the wrong side, then press the depth of the casing plus the depth of the frill over to the wrong side (**C**). Pin, then machine-stitch in place along the lower edge of the casing.

2. Stitch a second row about $\frac{3}{4}$–$1\frac{1}{4}$ in. above the first to form the casing channel (**D**).

C

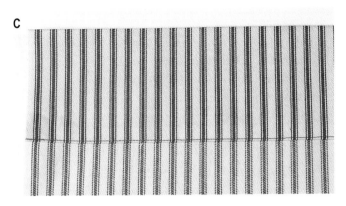

D

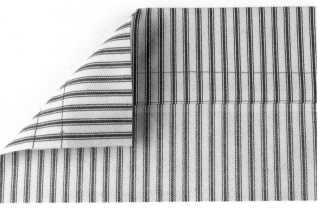

SEPARATE CASINGS

These casings have a separate strip cut to form the casing. The strip can be cut straight, or on the bias if it is to fit around a curved edge. Cut the strip the required depth of the casing plus $\frac{3}{4}$ in. on the length and 1 in. on the width.

1. Press $\frac{3}{8}$ in. to the wrong side at the two short ends and lower long edge of the casing strip. Place the casing to the edge of the garment with right sides facing and raw edges even. Pin, then stitch in place $\frac{5}{8}$ in. from the edge of the garment (**E**).

2. Press the casing over to the wrong side. Pin, and machine-stitch in place around the lower edge of the strip (**F**). Stitch a second row around just below the top edge to give it a neat finish.

E

F

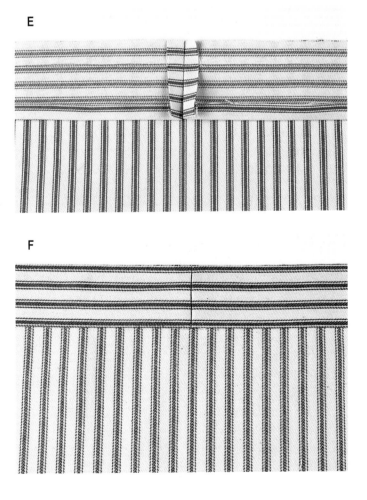

Drawstring Bag

Ideal for shoes, lingerie, or toys, this drawstring bag has a casing at the top edge, with a channel stitched down from the edge to form a self-frill at the top when the bag is pulled closed.

MATERIALS
½ yd. decorator or cotton fabric
2¼ yds. ribbon or cord

CUTTING OUT
1 Cut out two fabric pieces, both 13¾ in. wide by 19¾ in. deep.

STITCHING
1 Place the two pieces of fabric together with right sides together and raw edges even. Mark a ¾ in. opening about 5½–6¼ in. down from the top on both sides. This will allow for the side openings. Stitch the two pieces of fabric together around the side and base edges. Trim the corners and press the seams open.

NOTE
Ribbons and cords both make quick and easy drawstrings for a bag. Shoelaces could even be used to make a sporty shoe bag! To insert a ribbon into a casing, thread the ribbon onto a large-eyed, blunt needle, then pass the needle along through the casing to thread the ribbon in place. Alternatively, fasten a safety pin onto the end of a ribbon or cord and use it to hold onto while threading around the casing.

2 Press ⅜ in. to the wrong side around the top edge, then press 3 in over to the wrong side to form the casing. Stitch around the lower edge of the casing, then again ¾ in. above the first row to form the casing channel (**diagram 1**).

DIAGRAM 1

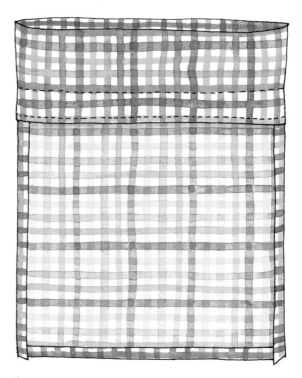

3 Turn the bag right-side out and press the seams at the edges. Cut the ribbon or cord into two equal lengths. Thread one length in through one side opening through the casing channel and back out the same opening. Knot the ends together. Thread the other length through the opposite opening in the same way. To stop the cords from pulling through, stitch at the center of the channel.

Mitered Corners and Borders

Mitering is a neat way to remove fullness from the corners on seams and hems. The miters can be formed and left unstitched to make neat corners on pocket seams, or they can be stitched, which they often are on deeper hems.

MITERING A CORNER

Press the seam allowance or hem to the wrong side on the two sides adjacent to the corner, then unfold the edges. Fold the corner in diagonally across the point where the two folds intersect and press (**A**). Trim the corner $\frac{3}{8}$ in. from the fold and refold the miter. Unstitched miters on fine fabrics can be trimmed closer.

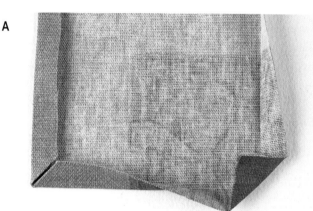

A

Stitching a mitered corner

Form the mitered corner as above and hand-stitch the mitered edges together on the pressed crease using a ladder stitch (**B**).

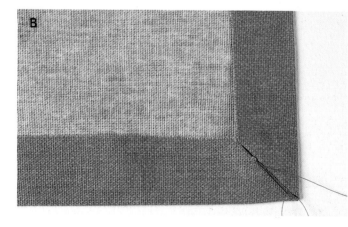

B

Double-mitered hem

1. Press the appropriate double hem in place, then unfold the outer fold. Fold the corner over diagonally, level with the inner pressed corner (**C**). Press the fold and trim the corner away $\frac{3}{8}$ in. inside the fold.

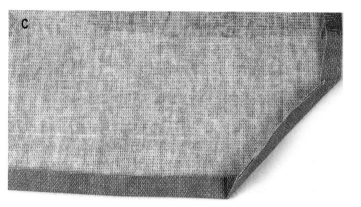

C

2. Refold the corners so the pressed lines match. Stitch on the pressed line from the corner to finish at the outer hem fold. Press the miter seam open (**D**). Refold the hem and press again. Alternatively, the formed miter can be ladder-stitched like the mitered corner.

D

DOUBLE-MITERED BORDER

1. Fold the borders in half, wrong sides out. Overlap the ends of two borders at right angles, with the fold edges on the outer edges and the ends, projecting by $\frac{5}{8}$ in., and pin. Draw a seam line diagonally across the corner between the points where the borders intersect (**E**).

E

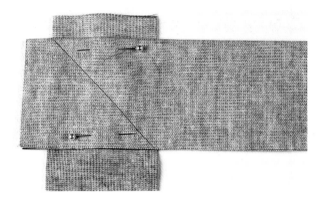

2. Mark the seam allowance $\frac{3}{8}$ in. outside the seam line. Turn the border over and repeat on the other side. Trim along the outer lines (**F**).

F

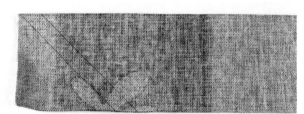

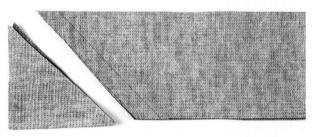

3. Unpin the borders, open them out, and mark the seamline on the unmarked half of each border. Place the appropriate two borders together with right sides together and stitch on the marked lines, starting and finishing $\frac{5}{8}$ in. in from the side edges of the border (**G**).

G

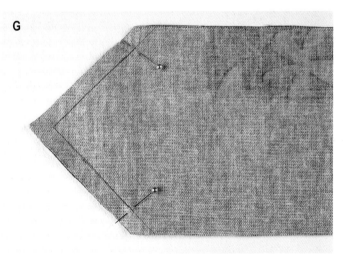

4. Trim the point and press the seam open. Stitch all four corners in this way. Turn the border right-side out. Fold the border in half with the wrong sides facing and press (**H**).

H

Tablecloth and Napkin

A gingham border adds a smart finishing touch to this pretty floral tablecloth and four matching napkins. The mitered double border is stitched first to the wrong side then to the right side, enclosing all the raw edges inside the border. This gives a neat finish and makes the garment strong enough for frequent laundering.

MATERIALS

Cotton fabric (for tablecloth and napkin panels)

Gingham fabric (for tablecloth and napkin borders)

CUTTING OUT

1 Cut out the cotton tablecloth fabric to the required finished size minus $5\frac{1}{8}$ in. (Seam allowances of $\frac{5}{8}$ in. are included). Cut the four gingham fabric borders the length of the cloth sides plus $6\frac{1}{4}$ x $7\frac{1}{4}$ in. wide.

2 Cut the eight napkin panels $13\frac{1}{2}$ in. square and the four gingham borders $17\frac{1}{4}$ x $5\frac{1}{8}$ in.

STITCHING

1 To make the tablecloth, stitch the short edges of the tablecloth borders together to make a double-mitered border. (See page 45.)

2 Mark the center of each edge of the cloth and the border with pins. Place one edge of the border to the wrong side of the cloth and pin together at the center pin with the raw edges even.

3 Match and pin at the corners so the end of the miter stitching is ⅝ in. from the edge of the cloth at each corner (**diagram 1**). Pin between the corners and center pins and then baste. Stitch the border in place, stopping and restarting at each corner.

DIAGRAM 1

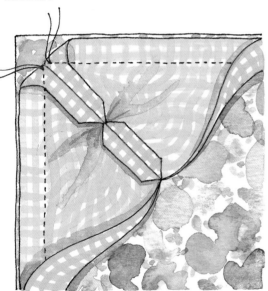

4 Press ⅝ in. to the wrong side around the edges of the remaining border and place this edge onto the right side of the cloth so all the raw edges are enclosed. Pin, then machine-stitch in place on the right side (**diagram 2**). The finished border will be 3¼ in. wide.

5 Make the napkins in the same way as the tablecloth. The napkin borders will be 2 in. wide.

DIAGRAM 2

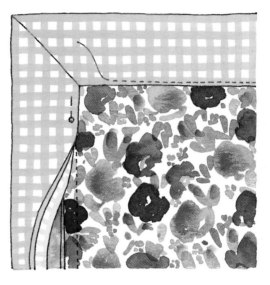

Table Runner with Mitered Border

This silk table runner has an organza mitered border, making it a gorgeous centerpiece for any table. The measurements given will make a runner with a $10\frac{1}{4}$-in.-wide center panel and $2\frac{3}{4}$-in. borders.

MATERIALS
Silk dupion fabric for center panel
(amount as required)
Organza fabric (amount as required)
Erasable vanish-pen
Ruler

CUTTING OUT

1 To estimate the length of the center panel, measure the total length of the table and subtract $4\frac{1}{4}$ in. Cut out two center panels $11\frac{1}{2}$ in. wide by the required length. Allow $\frac{5}{8}$ in. for seams.

2 For the short ends of the border, cut organza strips $6\frac{3}{4}$ in. wide x 17 in. Cut organza strips for the long edges the same width and by the cut length of the center panel plus $5\frac{1}{2}$ in.

STITCHING

1 Stitch the borders together to form a long, rectangular double-mitered border (**diagram 1**). (See page 45 for making double-mitered borders).

DIAGRAM 1

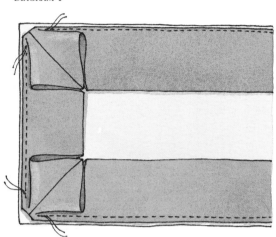

2 Treating the two layers of the border as one, mark the center of the raw border edges and the edges of one center panel with pins. With right sides together and raw edges even, place the border around the edge of one center panel. Match and pin to join the border and panel in the center.

3 Match and pin at the corners so the end of the miter stitching is ⅝ in. from the edges of the panel at each corner. Pin between the corners and center pins. Stitch the border in place, stopping and restarting the stitching neatly at each corner.

4 Press ⅝ in. to the wrong side around the edges of the remaining center panel piece. Place to the wrong side of the stitched panel so that its edges are even with the previous stitching and all raw edges are enclosed. Handstitch in place into the back of the previous stitching (**diagram 2**).

DIAGRAM 2

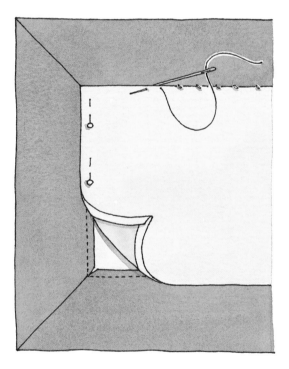

Table Runner with Two Borders

Coordinated country checks and stripes make a chic table runner with a double-mitered border. Cut the center panel 10 in. narrower than the width you require for the finished runner, and cut the first single borders to the length of the panel edges plus $5\frac{1}{2}$ x 4 in. Stitch the single borders to the center panel, finishing the stitching $\frac{5}{8}$ in. from each corner. One by one, fold each corner diagonally so the two borders are even. Draw the miter line across the border in line with the diagonal fold on the center panel. Stitch the borders together along the line, trim away the excess fabric, then stitch on the outer double-mitered border.

Fastenings

Zippers, buttons, and other fastenings join edges together in a temporary way so an item can be opened and re-fastened easily. While fastenings serve an obvious functional purpose, many can be used for decorative effect.

ZIPPERS

Zippers are available in a range of colors and sizes, and also in different weights. Zipper lengths are sized at 2-in. intervals. The zipper length refers to the length of the zipper teeth. Most zippers will have extra zipper tape protruding beyond the teeth at each end for stitching a neat finish. There are a number of different types of zippers:

Chain zipper The standard medium-weight, multipurpose zipper with plastic or metal teeth on a woven tape.

Coil zipper A lightweight zipper with the opening part formed by nylon or polyester coils attached to a woven tape.

Concealed zipper A specialist type of coil zipper with the coiled teeth concealed behind the zipper tape. These zippers can only be inserted using a concealed zipper machine foot.

Open-ended zippers A heavyweight zipper with metal or plastic teeth that can be separated at the base to form two halves.

Positioning zippers in seams

Zippers placed in seams will have a seam continuing at each end of the zipper. This method is used mainly on cushion covers.

1. Stitch with a plain seam, leaving an opening the length of the zipper teeth plus $\frac{1}{4}$ in. (**A**).

2. Press the seam open, continuing to press the seam allowances to the wrong side along the open part in preparation for inserting the zipper. When inserting the zipper, arrange it centrally within the opening.

A

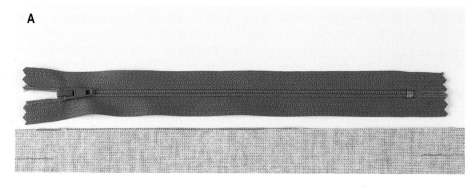

Positioning zippers in waistbands

Zippers that finish into waistbands have a seam at the lower ends of the zipper only, and can open at the top.

1. Stitch with a plain seam first, leaving an opening the length of the zipper teeth plus $\frac{3}{4}$ in. for the seam allowance at the waist edge (**B**).

2. Press the seam open, continuing to press the seam allowances to the wrong side along the open part in preparation for inserting the zipper. When inserting the zipper, arrange the lower end of the zipper teeth at the base of the opening.

B

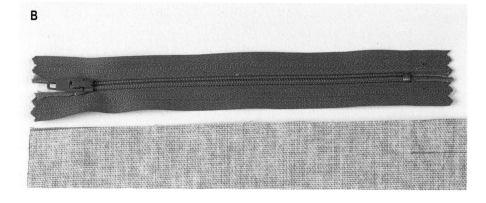

Inserting a lapped zipper

A lapped zipper has one fabric edge lapped over to cover the zipper. This method can be used for positioning a lapped zipper in a seam as well as into a waistband.

1. Working with right sides uppermost, pin and tack the zipper behind the opening so the right-hand edge of the opening is just outside the zipper teeth. Using a zipper machine foot, stitch in place near the edge. Begin stitching with the zipper partway open, then stop with the needle down, slide the zipper past the needle, and complete the stitching (**C**).

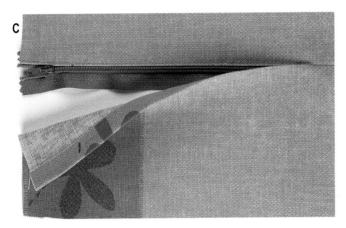

2. Arrange the other edge of the opening even with the stitching. Pin, then baste this edge about $\frac{3}{8}$ in. from the zipper tape. Stitch along the long edge again, starting with the zipper partway open in the same way as with the first edge. At the end of the zipper, stitch across at an angle to finish neatly (**D**).

Exposed zipper

This easy method exposes the zipper teeth and some of the tape for a decorative effect. No stitching is visible on the right side. This method is only suitable for joining two separate edges that are not seamed together at either end of the zipper. Arrange the zipper centrally on the fabric edge, with the right sides facing and the zipper tape nearest the fabric edge. Pin and tack the zipper tape to the fabric $\frac{5}{8}$ in. from the edge. Machine-stitch in place. Stitch the other edge of the fabric to the other edge of the zipper in the same way.

BUTTONS

There are two main types of buttons: flat buttons, which have two or four holes pierced through them from the front to the back, and shank buttons, which are stitched on by a protruding shank at the back. A shank spaces the button away from the fabric to allow fabric layers to lie flat under the button when it is fastened. The thicker the fabric, the longer the shank needs to be. Stitch buttons on with doubled thread for strength.

Stitching on flat buttons

To sew on a button with two holes, fasten it onto the fabric with a few backstitches on the wrong side. Bring the needle up through one hole in the button, then back down the other hole and through the fabric. Work four to six stitches in this way to secure, then fasten off with backstitches behind the button. On buttons with four holes, work two parallel sets of stitches (**E**), or form the stitches into a cross.

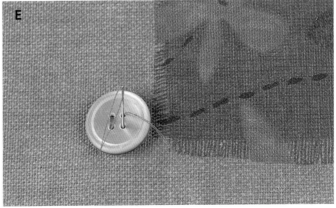

Making a shank for a flat button

1. Stitch on the button in the same way as for a button with holes, but stitch over a toothpick or a thick needle placed on top of the button as a spacer (**F**).

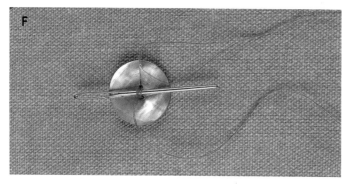

2. Before finishing off, take the thread through between the button and the fabric. Remove the spacer and wind the thread around the stitches between the button and fabric to form a thread shank (**G**). Fasten off.

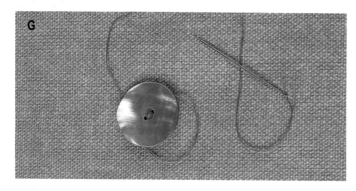

Stitching on a shank button

Fasten the thread on the fabric with a few backstitches on the wrong side. Stitch alternately through the shank and the fabric four to six times, then fasten off with backstitches on the wrong side behind the button (**H**).

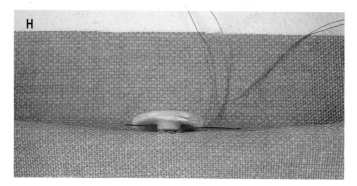

Fabric-covered buttons

Plastic and metal molds for making your own covered buttons are available in kit form.

1. To cover a button, first cut out a circle of fabric to the size given on the button packet. Stitch a small running stitch around the edge of the circle. Place the button front onto the fabric circle and pull up the running stitches to gather the circle in (**I**).

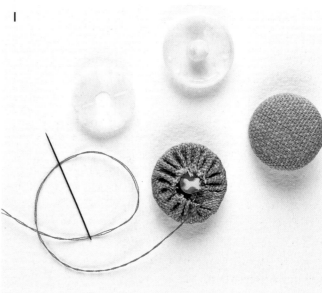

2. Arrange the fabric so that the button is covered smoothly, fasten off the thread, and push the button back onto the front to clip the two pieces together.

Some types of covered buttons do not need gathering; these have little metal hooks inside the rim of the button mold. Pull the edge of the fabric circle onto the hooks first on two opposite edges, then onto the other two opposite edges. Then, unhooking and rehooking when necessary, hook on the areas in between. When the circle is fastened in place, smoothly clip the back on.

MAKING BUTTONHOLES

Buttonholes are quick and easy to make using a sewing machine. The exact method varies according to the machine model and will be explained in the machine's manual.

Buttonholes are stitched with a close zigzag stitch, with a wide stitch at each end called a bar tack, and stitches half as wide along each side of the buttonhole (**J**). To establish the length of the buttonhole, add the depth of the button to its diameter. Always make a test buttonhole on spare fabric first to test the size.

Cut the buttonhole along the center after stitching using small scissors. Cut from each end toward the center.

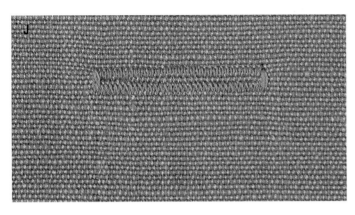

Handstitched buttonholes

Handstitched buttonholes are usually made with one round end, where the button will sit, and one square end. If the holes are being made for ribbon or cord slots, they can be made with two round or two square ends. Work the buttonhole stitching using ordinary sewing thread.

1. Mark the center and length of the buttonhole with a line. Stitch a small rectangle of running- or machine-stitch $\frac{1}{8}$ in. away around the line to mark the outside of the stitching. Carefully cut the buttonhole (**K**).

2. Secure a thread at the lower left-hand corner at the square end of the buttonhole. Bring the needle through from back to front just outside the stitched line and pass it under the point of the needle from left to right (**L**). Pull the needle through and draw the thread upward so the knot that has formed sits on the fabric edge. Work stitches in this way close together along to the round end of the buttonhole.

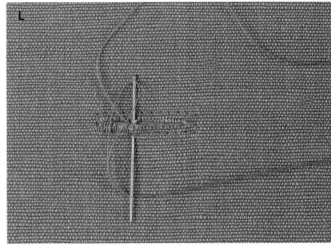

3. At the round end, work seven stitches radiating around the end. Turn the work and stitch back along the other straight edge (**M**). On the last stitch, pass the needle through the knot of the first stitch and out at the base of the last stitch to pull the two edges together. Stitch two long stitches across the length of the square end, then turn the work and stitch the square end with the knots of the stitches toward the buttonhole.

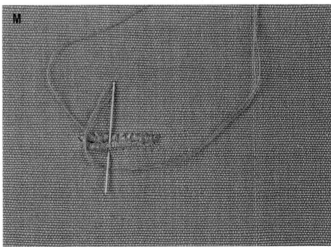

HOOKS AND EYES

Hooks and eyes are used to fasten two butting edges. Use double thread for strength and position the hook toward the edge with its end $\frac{1}{8}$ in. from the edge.

Stitch around over each hole on the hook without stitching through to the right side, then stitch two or three stitches over the neck of the hook to secure it. Position the eye to match so it projects $\frac{1}{8}$ in. over the fabric edge. Stitch around each hole, then over each side edge of the eye (**N**).

HOOKS AND BARS

Hooks and bars, or straight eyes, are used to fasten two overlapping edges, such as on a waistband. For a bar or straight eye, mark its position with a pin to match the hook. Stitch around the first hole of the bar, then slip the needle between the fabric layers to the other hole and stitch around that. Two hooks and bars are often stitched side by side to fasten a waistband (**O**).

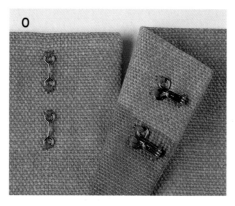

PRESS STUDS

Press stud fasteners are used to make a small, fairly lightweight fastening. They are available in a good range of sizes, and in silver, black, or clear plastic. One half of the fastener has a ball, and the other a socket which clips the two halves together.

Using double thread, stitch the ball half of the stud to the overlapping edge with three or four stitches through each of the holes around the stud. Close the opening and pass a pin through the hole at the center of the stud to mark the position for the other half, then stitch the socket half in place in the same way as before (**P**).

Non-sew stud fastenings

Available in a range of styles and sizes, non-sew studs can make fairly sturdy fastenings. They are usually hammered or snapped in place with tools provided with the kit, or purchased separately. These fasteners usually have a decorative cap, and the top layer of fabric is held between this and the socket. The ball half is then attached to the other fabric layer with a rivet on the wrong side.

VELCRO™

Sometimes called touch and close fastener, Velcro™ has two halves: one is covered in tiny soft loops, and the other is covered with minute hooks that fasten onto the loops firmly when the halves are pushed together (**Q**). Velcro™ is available in strip form for fastening long edges, and also in small, round spots for joining overlapping edges. Velcro™ is also available with one sewable side and one adhesive side, which is useful for attaching fabric or blinds to a frame.

Stitch Velcro™ in place along the flat areas at the edge by machine or by hand, hemstitching over the edge.

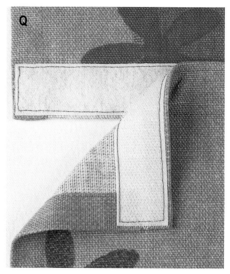

Buttoned Pillow

This pillow has two panels at the front. Each panel is finished with a deep hem that overlaps and is fastened together with buttons. This design creates a useful opening for the pillow pad as well as a decorative feature.

MATERIALS

1 yd. decorator or cotton fabric
Three $\frac{3}{4}$-in. buttons
Pillow form, 16 in. square

CUTTING OUT

1 Cut two pieces of fabric for the front of the pillow, one $14\frac{3}{8}$ x 17 in. and one $8\frac{3}{4}$ x 17 in. Cut a piece for the back as well that is 17 in. squared. This measurement includes $\frac{5}{8}$ in. seam allowances.

STITCHING

1 Press $\frac{3}{8}$ in. then $1\frac{3}{4}$ in. hems to the wrong side along one 17 in. long edge on each front piece. Machine-stitch in place.

2 Mark three buttonhole positions on the hem of the narrower front piece, one at the center, then two others 4 in. on either side. Mark the buttonholes at right angles to the hem edge and beginning $\frac{5}{8}$ in. in from the hem edge, making sure they are long enough to fit the buttons. Stitch and then cut the buttonholes.

3 Overlap the two hems with right sides uppermost and the buttonhole hem on top. Mark the buttons' positions on the underside and stitch them in place (**diagram 1**).

DIAGRAM 1

4 Fasten the buttons. Place the back piece of the pillow to the front with right sides facing and raw edges level and stitch together around the outer edges, leaving a $\frac{5}{8}$-in. seam all around. Trim the corners and press the seams open as far as possible. Unfasten the buttons, turn the cover right-side out, and press the seam at the edge.

Moving buttons

Unpick the button, then place the buttonhole where the new fastening is required. Pin through the end of the buttonhole to mark the new button position. Carefully pull away the buttonhole, leaving the pin in place. Stitch the button onto the new position, remembering to make a thread shank if required. (See page 56.)

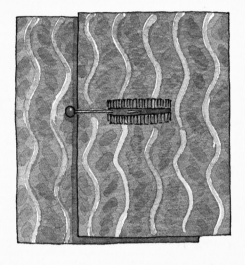

TORN BUTTONS
Buttons can get pulled off, taking a piece of fabric with them. The fabric will need to be repaired before the button can be restitched. To do this, cut a circle of mending tape a little smaller than the button. Iron it to the wrong side of the button position. On the right side, work rows of machine-stitch or hand running stitch backward and forward across the circle to reinforce the area. Restitch the button in place.

Zip-Up Bags

Neat zip-up bags can serve a number of purposes. Here, we show you how to make a zip-up bag that can be easily used to hold cosmetics or toiletries. Iron-on interfacing is added to give extra body to the fabric. For a durable, wipe-clean finish, you can also add optional lining made from shower-curtain lining fabric.

MATERIALS

$\frac{5}{8}$ yd. decorator or cotton fabric
$\frac{5}{8}$ yd. iron-on interfacing
8-in. zipper
Shower-curtain lining fabric (optional)

CUTTING OUT

1 To make a small cosmetics bag, cut two pieces of fabric to 7 x 9$\frac{1}{2}$ in. Cut two pieces the same size from the interfacing. Seam allowances measuring $\frac{5}{8}$ in. are included.

Large toiletries bag

Larger bags can be made in this way as well. To make the toiletry bag shown on page 65, you will need two pieces of fabric measuring 11 x 13$\frac{1}{2}$ in., the same amount of interfacing, and a 12-in. zipper. Make in the same way as you did the small cosmetics bag.

STITCHING

1 Apply the interfacing to the wrong side of the fabric panels. Stitch the zipper to the center of the two long top edges using the exposed zipper method. (See page 55.)

2 With right sides together, raw edges even and the zipper partly open, stitch the two bag pieces together around the side and bottom edges. Press the seams open (**diagram 1**).

DIAGRAM 1

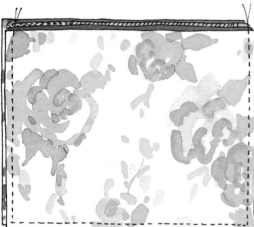

3 Separate two layers at the lower corners and refold them diagonally, so that the side and bottom seams are on top of each other at the center of the point. Stitch across at

right angles to the seams $1\frac{3}{4}$ in. from the points (**diagram 2**). Trim the point away $\frac{3}{8}$ in. above the stitching. Turn the bag right-side out.

DIAGRAM 2

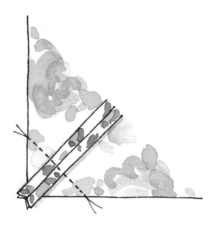

4 To make an optional lining, cut two pieces of lining fabric to the same size as the bag. Sew the lining bag together as you did the outer fabric bag. Place the lining inside the bag, right side facing out. Tuck it under the raw edge of the lining around the top edge, level with the zipper stitching. Handstitch the lining to the back of the zipper stitching.

Replacing a Zipper

When replacing a zipper, the first thing to do is to note the way the original zipper was stitched, so that the replacement zipper can be stitched in the same way. First, unpick the zipper as far as possible. While unpicking, you may encounter difficulty where the ends of the zipper tape are stitched inside the waistband or collar. Often the best solution to this problem is to snip through the zipper tape, leaving the ends inside the waistband, then pin and baste the new zipper in place.

Sometimes it is possible to unpick a few stitches at the waistband and to tuck the ends of the zipper tape in before restitching. If this is not possible, however, fold the ends of the zipper tape back at an angle, as shown, then stitch the zipper in place and handstitch the folded back tape.

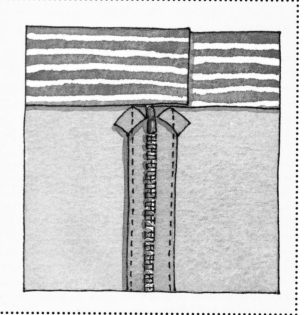

Piping, Gathers, and Pleats

There are many ways to apply decorative finishes to sewn items—piping, gathers, and pleats all add interest in different ways.

PIPING

Piping can be bought readymade with a projecting flange to insert in a seam, or it can be made by covering piping cord with a strip of bias-cut fabric to match your item. Covering piping with checked and striped fabrics can be especially effective.

Cutting bias strips

Fold the fabric diagonally so the cross-grain is even with, or parallel to the selvages. (See page 12.) Cut along the diagonal fold, and then cut the bias strips along the cut edge, making them wide enough to cover the cord plus two ⅝-in. seam allowances.

Joining the strips

1. If a long bias strip is required, trim the two ends on the straight grain. Place the two ends together with right sides together, the straight ends even, and the fold lines intersecting ¼ in. Pin to hold.

2. Stitch the two ends together, taking a ¼-in. seam (**A**). Press the seam open. Trim the seam corners even with the edge.

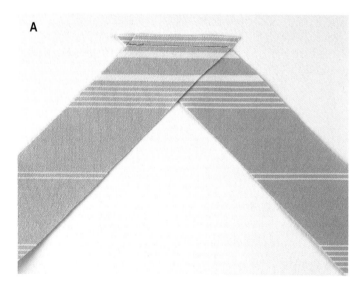

A

Covering piping cord

Place the cord at the center of the bias strip and wrap the strip around the cord so that the raw edges of the strip are even. Using the zipper foot on your sewing machine, baste along the flat area (flange) close to the cord, but not right next to it (**B**).

B

Joining ends

1. Stitch the piping in place to the right side of the fabric, keeping the raw edges even and stitching along the line of the previous stitching. Leave about 1 in. unstitched at each end of the piping.

2. Cut the piping so it overlaps the first end by 1 in. Unpick the end of the piping to reveal the cord and snip away the cord even with the facing cord.

3. Fold the raw edges under on the overlapping end and lap it over the beginning. Complete the stitching (**C**).

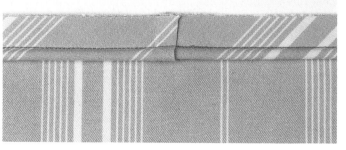

C

Finishing ends

At the end of a strip of piping, snip away the cord only at the finishing point, leaving some of the bias strip fabric intact. Fold the end of the bias strip diagonally across into the seam allowance and stitch into place (**D**).

D

Curves and corners

When you are attaching piping that goes around corners, you will need to snip into the flat area $\frac{5}{8}$ in. from the corner, so it will open out to fit around the corner with the raw edges even with the next edge (**E**). On most curved seams the bias cut strip has enough give to fit around without the need to snip, but if it does not, snip at intervals.

E

Using readymade piping

There are two types of readymade piping: one has an inner cord covered by fabric, which can be stitched in the same way as piping you have made yourself. The other type has no inner cord, just a cord woven onto an attached flat area.

When joining ends of the latter type, it is best to overlap the ends diagonally into the seam allowance (**F**). Leave the piping unstitched for a little way on each side of the join. Press the overlapping ends as flat as they'll go, or if possible, unravel the ends of the piping to flatten it where it goes into the seam. Overlap the ends diagonally into the seam allowance and complete the stitching.

F

GATHERS

Gathers, which take in fullness, are often used to form a frill, a skirt, or a curtain. Less formal gathers are usually formed along the entire edge, while more tailored pleats can be repeated, spaced at intervals, or made at corners. For gathers, allow one and a half times the required finished length of fabric.

Stitching a gather

Gathered stitching can be done by hand, using running stitch, or by machine. Using a machine is quicker and will produce more even gathers. A single row of gathering stitches can be worked along the seamline, but a double row will allow the fabric to hang more neatly.

1. Adjust the machine stitch to its longest length and stitch along $\frac{5}{8}$ in. from the edge, leaving the threads ends. Stitch a second row of gathering $\frac{1}{4}$ in. above the first row. On long frills, stop and restart the stitching to divide the gathered edge up into about 30 in. lengths (**G**).

G

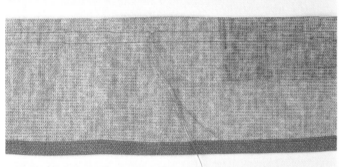

Attaching a gather frill

1. Divide the frill and the edge it is to be stitched to into an equal number of sections and mark with pins. Pin the two edges together with right sides facing at the marker pins. Pull both the gathering threads on the wrong side of the frill together while sliding the fabric along to form a gathered frill (**H**).

H

2. When the gathers fit, wind the thread ends around a pin in a figure of eight to hold. Adjust the gathers evenly, then pin and stitch in place just below the seamline (**I**).

I

PLEATS

Pleats can be pressed to give a sharp crease down the length of the pleat, or they can be left unpressed so that the pleats are held at the top edge only for a less formal look. To make pleats, allow twice as much fabric as the required finished width.

Knife pleats

These are a series of single pleats facing in the same direction, usually toward the right.

1. Measure and mark the depth of the required pleats at the top edge, and at intervals down the length using pins or an erasable marker pen.

2. Fold one marking over to meet the other to form the pleats. Press the pleats, removing the pins as you reach them. Pin along the seamline at the top edge. If making rows of pleats, machine-baste across the top edge to hold them in place (**J**).

Box pleats

Box pleats are formed by creating two pleats facing away from each other (**K**). Measure and mark the depth of the pleats required at the top edge and at intervals down the length with pins or an erasable marker pen. Fold the two inner markings outward, away from each other to meet the outer markings. Press the pleats, removing the pins as you reach them. Pin along the seamline at the top edge.

If making rows of pleats, machine-baste across the top edge to hold the pleats in place.

Inverted pleats

These are formed from two pleats facing toward each other so that the two folds meet at the center.

1. Measure and mark the depth of the required pleats at the top edge and at intervals down the length with pins or an erasable marker pen.

2. Fold the two outer markings inward toward each other to meet at the center marking. Press the pleats, removing the pins as you reach them. Pin along the seam line at the top edge (**L**). If making rows of pleats, machine-baste across the top edge to hold the pleats in place.

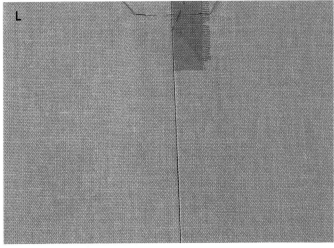

Chair-Seat Cover

**Smartly striped in cool, neutral shades, this
elegant seat cover will add charm to a simple
dining chair. The skirt cover follows the
stripes to make the pleats, and is finished at
the top with a neat piping in the seam.**

MATERIALS
Pattern paper
Pencil
$1\frac{1}{4}$ yd. furnishing fabric
$1\frac{3}{4}$ yd. piping cord

CUTTING OUT

1 Lay the pattern paper on the chair seat
and draw the seat outline. Add $\frac{5}{8}$ in. to the
side and front edges and $1\frac{1}{4}$ in. to the back
edge for seam allowances. Cut out.

2 Measure around the side and front edge
of the seat pattern and cut the skirt
approximately twice that length, allowing an
extra 9 in. where the skirt pieces are joined.

3 Cut a strip of extra fabric on the bias to
cover the piping. You will need to measure
around the seat for the amount required. Cut
fabric for four ties, each $1\frac{1}{2}$ in. x $15\frac{3}{4}$ in.

STITCHING

1 Cover the piping cord with the bias strip.
Stitch the piping around the chair seat, finishing the ends of the piping $1\frac{1}{4}$ in. from the
back edge.

2 Press a $\frac{3}{8}$-in. then a 1-in. hem to the
wrong side along the lower edge of the skirt.

3 Form and press the skirt pleats, if possible
using the fabric stripes as a guide. For the
pleats shown here, $1\frac{1}{2}$ in. is taken out in each
pleat, and the crease of each pleat is $1\frac{1}{2}$ in.
from the following one (**diagram 1**). Allow at
least $2\frac{1}{4}$ in. of fabric to be free from pleats at
each end.

DIAGRAM 1

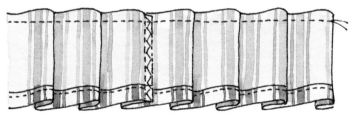

4 Join the skirt pieces at the inside fold of the pleat by stitching the seam through both fabric and hem. Press the pleats at the complete length required, then pin and machine-stitch the pleats in place $\frac{5}{8}$ in. down from the top edge.

DIAGRAM 2

5 Pin the skirt in place around the seat with right sides together and the raw edges and the back edges even. Stitch in place just inside the piping stitching (**diagram 2**).

6 Press $\frac{3}{8}$ in. then $\frac{3}{8}$ in. to the wrong side along the back edges of the skirt and seat. Machine-stitch in place, stopping and restarting the stitching at the piped seam.

7 To make the ties, press $\frac{3}{8}$ in. to the wrong side along the two long edges and one short edge of each tie piece. Press each in half so the raw edges are enclosed and machine-stitch down the long edge. Place the cover on the chair and pin the ends of the ties in position under the hem at the top of the skirt and on the back edge to fasten around the back uprights. Remove the chair cover and stitch the ties in place.

Pretty Paisley Chair-Seat Cover Variation

This pretty variation of the chair seat cover has a gathered skirt, contrast piping, and cut-out back corners to accommodate the chair back's uprights. Paisley print fabric is teamed up with a plain 1 in. bias binding to finish the cutout back corners and to cover the piping cord.

Cut out the fabric, allowing one and a half times the finished length for the gathered skirt. Bind the corners with the bias binding, making little mitered pleats at the inner corners. Open out the remaining bias binding, press it flat, and use it to cover the piping cord. Make up the cover, gathering the skirt to fit around the side and front edges.

Finishing Touches

Decorative touches will add designer details to simple projects in a surprisingly quick and easy way. An appliqué motif personalizes an item, elegant bows add a bold impact, and a handstitched fringe adds a discreet but stylish detail.

BOWS

1. Cut a strip of fabric twice the required width plus ¾ in. Fold the strip in half lengthwise and tie into a bow to establish the required length, allowing an extra ¾ in. for seams. Untie the bow. Fold the strip in half lengthwise with right sides facing and raw edges level. Stitch along the two short edges and the long edge ⅜ in. from the edge, leaving an opening at the center of the long edge for an opening (**A**).

A

2. Trim the corners and turn the strip right-side out. Press the seams at the edge, stitch the opening closed and tie into a bow (**B**).

B

TIES

Cut the ties to the required finished length plus ¾ in., and twice the width plus ¾ in. Press ⅜ in. to the wrong side across one short end (or both if they show) and the two long edges. Press the tie in half lengthwise. Tack, then stitch down the long edge and across the pressed end (**C**).

C

APPLYING LACE AND BRAID

Lace and braids can be stitched to the surface of fabric or to the edge by hand or machine. If you are attaching braid to the surface of the fabric, pin the braid in place, then stitch in place by hand with running stitch, backstitch or small hem stitches over the edge. Alternatively, machine-stitch with straight or zigzag stitches. When applying lace or braid to a fabric edge, a neat finish is obtained when the raw edge is folded to the wrong side first so the zigzag stitching attaches the lace and neatens the fabric edge at the same time (**D**).

D

STITCHING CORD

Cords give a finished look when they are stitched to the edge of items such as cushions. Hold the cord in place with one hand and stitch with the other, taking a small straight stitch through the underside of the cord, then a longer diagonal stitch through the fabric from one side to the other (**E**).

E

HEMSTITCHED FRINGE

This type of hemstitching is a form of counted thread work and is different from ordinary hemstitching. It is best worked on an even-weave fabric so the threads can be counted.

1. Pull out a few threads along where the fringe's top will be. Working right to left along the top edge of the fringe, bring the needle out a few threads in from the drawn threads.

2. Take the needle up to the pulled thread and pass it through behind a bunch of four threads. Pull through, reinsert the needle at the start of the four threads and bring it out level with the end of the bunch. Repeat (**F**).

3. When the hemstitching is complete, pull the threads away to form the fringe.

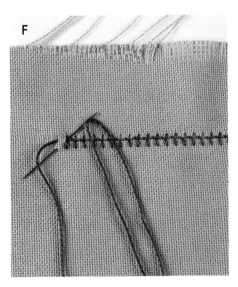

EMBROIDERY STITCHES
Blanket stitch

This stitch is often worked at the edge of a fabric to give a decorative finish. It can also be worked at the edges of appliqué shapes.

1. Working from left to right, bring the needle out at the lower edge of the stitch, insert it at the top of the stitch and bring it out at the bottom with the thread under the needlepoint.

2. Pull the needle through to form a loop. Move the needle along to the right and repeat (**G**).

Chain stitch

1. Working so the stitches are coming toward you, bring the needle out at the top of the line and hold the thread down with your left thumb.

2. Insert the needle where it last came out and bring the point out a short distance away, then pull the needle through, keeping the thread under the needle to form the loop.

Insert the needle where it last came out and continue. Single chain stitches can be worked to make a daisy stitch by taking a small stitch over the end of the formed loop (**H**).

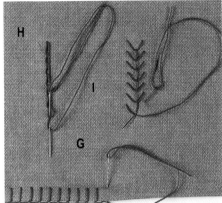

Fly stitch

Bring the needle through at the top left, holding it down with your left thumb. Insert the needle across to the right at the same level and bring it out diagonally downward centrally between the top two stitches. Take a straight stitch downward and repeat (**I**).

APPLIQUÉ

Appliqué is the application of cutout fabric shapes to other pieces of fabric to make a design or pattern. The process is made wonderfully easy by the use of a special backing fabric called "fusible web," which fuses onto the fabric shape to be appliquéd. This prevents the edges from fraying and does away with the need to tack.

Making an appliqué shape

Draw out or trace your chosen design onto paper, then trace it onto the paper side of the fusible web. (If you are using fusible web, the design will be reversed, so if the design has an obvious left or right, you will need to draw the design in reverse). Cut out the shapes roughly and apply the fusible web to the wrong side of the appliqué fabric. Cut out the pieces, then peel off the paper backing (**J**). Arrange the appliqué pieces onto your fabric and iron them in place following the manufacturer's instructions.

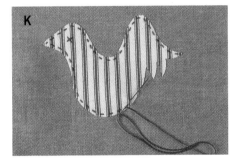

Edging an appliqué shape

With fusible web you don't need to stitch around the pieces, but doing so can add definition. Stitch a simple running stitch (**K**) or a blanket stitch just inside the edge. Be sure to buy lightweight or heavyweight fusible web according to project use.

Zigzag stitching appliqué

Zigzag stitching is another decorative option. Adjust the machine to a medium-width, close zigzag stitch and stitch around the appliquéd shapes. When stitching curves, stop every few stitches with the needle down on the outer edge of the curve, raise the presser foot and turn the fabric slightly to realign the edge. On inner curves, stop with the needle down on the inner curve. Tie off all thread ends on the wrong side to finish (**L**).

Pockets and Patches

Pockets make useful storage spaces. They can be added to many sewn items, including clothing, bags, chair arm covers, and wall organizers. A pocket can also act as a patch when it is used to cover a repaired tear or hole. Traditional patches are used to repair torn garments. If you cannot find a good fabric match to make a concealed repair, consider a contrasting or patterned fabric to add a decorative feature.

POCKETS

There are two types of simple pockets that can be added to sewn items: one is a patch pocket and the other is a pocket with gussets. A patch pocket is a flat piece of fabric stitched in place around three sides. It is commonly used on clothes and on the outside and inside of bags. A pocket with gussets has a concealed pleat of extra fabric down both sides of the pocket to provide more space inside the pockets. This type of pocket is usually used on wall hangings, where larger items may be stored.

Patch pockets

Patch pockets are usually made from rectangles or squares of fabric.

1. Decide on the required finished size and add a $\frac{5}{8}$-in. seam allowance to the side and lower edges and a hem allowance of $1\frac{1}{4}$ in. at the top. Press the seam allowance to the wrong side around the side and lower edges. At the top edge, press $\frac{3}{8}$ in., then another

$\frac{3}{4}$ in. to the wrong side (**A**). Alternatively, on thicker fabric, zigzag stitch the top edge and fold down a single hem.

A

2. Place the pocket in the required position and pin in place. The pins are best placed at right angles to the edges and diagonally into the lower corners.

3. To sew the pocket onto the garment, start with back stitching at one top corner, then continue to stitch down one side, across the bottom and up the other side (**B**). Finish with back stitching to secure the pocket.

B

Pockets with gussets

1. Decide on the pocket size in the same way as for the patch pocket. (See left.) Then add on a gusset allowance, for example $1\frac{1}{2}$ in., to each side edge. This may make the cut piece of fabric wider than it is tall even though the finished pocket will be taller than it is wide. Make the pocket in the same way as the patch pocket.

2. Press 1½ in. to the wrong side down the side edge, then press the edge back level with the fold to make a ¾-in.-wide pleat under each side edge (**C**).

C

3. Place the pocket in position, lift the gusset fold carefully, and pin the side edges in place. Open the gusset out and pin, then stitch the side edges only.

4. Refold the gussets and stitch across the bottom of the pocket through all layers. Remember to start and finish with back stitching (**D**).

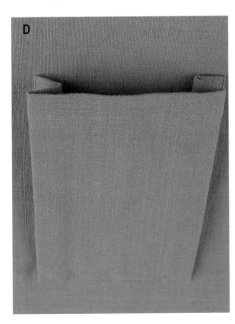

D

Divided pockets

A divided pocket can add an individual touch to a plain patch pocket; the divided section looks attractive and can be made to fit items such as small pens and notebooks, lipsticks, a toothbrush, or silverware in a silverware roll.

1. Decide on the required finished size for the entire pocket and add seams and hems as for the patch pocket. (See opposite.) Cut out and stitch the pocket on the garment in the same way as the patch pocket. (See opposite.)

2. Mark and pin the sections you want to divide and check that your items will fit snugly. Stitch the sections from the top to bottom either by following the line of the pins, removing them as you reach them, or by drawing a line with an erasable marker to stitch along (**E**).

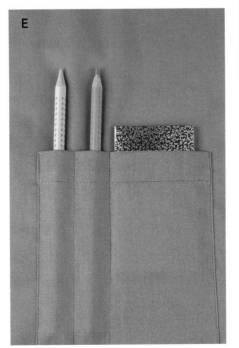

E

Mending a torn pocket

A torn top corner is one of the most common pocket repairs needed, particularly on utility items such as overalls or aprons, where the pockets can get caught on handles or hooks. Sometimes the stitching just gives, but more often the fabric behind the pocket tears.

1. First reinforce the tear area with a square of fabric, iron-on mending tape, or lightweight iron-on interfacing. You will need to cut a piece about ⅜ in. larger than the size of the tear. Pin or iron-on the reinforcing fabric to the wrong side of the tear, ensuring that the edges meet neatly.

2. Using a matching thread, stitch along the tear with a three-step zigzag or with small running stitches worked backward and forward across the tear in a tight zigzag formation (**F**).

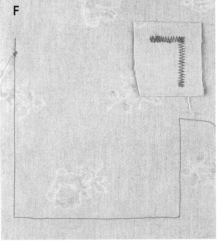

F

3. Trim away any excess fabric on the wrong side and restitch the pocket (**G**).

G

PATCHES

Patches are typically used to mend or cover tears, holes, and worn areas, but sometimes they are added to a garment solely as a decorative feature.

Handstitched patch

This method works well for light-to-medium-weight fabric tears and holes. If you can match the fabric pattern, the patch can be almost invisible. Larger repairs, such as on sheets, can be machine-stitched for greater ease if preferred.

1. Trim the worn or torn area to a square or rectangle. Snip a short, diagonal cut into each corner and press the raw edges to the wrong side around the hole (**H**).

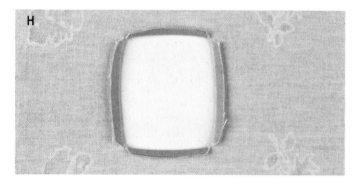

2. Cut a patch ¾–1 in. larger than the hole and press the raw edge to the right side around its edges (**I**).

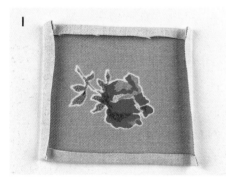

3. Place the patch to wrong side of the hole. Handstitch in place around the outer edge of the patch, taking small stitches through the main fabric. Turn to the right side and hand-stitch around the hole to the patch, this time making small stitches on the right side (**J**).

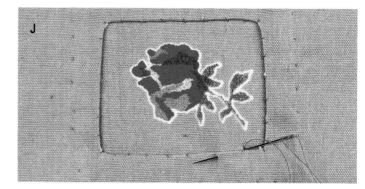

Zigzag-stitched patch

This robust method is suited to thick fabrics such as heavyweight denim, where the hand-stitched method would be too bulky. The patch will be functional, but not invisible.

1. Trim the tear or worn area to a neat oval shape (**K**). Cut the trimmed hole size from the center of a piece of fusible web.

2. Apply the fusible web to the wrong side of the patch fabric following the manufacturer's instructions. Cut out a patch ¾ in. larger than the hole (**L**).

3. Steam press to fuse the patch in place. Zigzag stitch around the outer edge of the patch with a wide, close stitch (**M**). If fusible web is not available, the same method can still be used, but you will need to zigzag stitch around the hole as well.

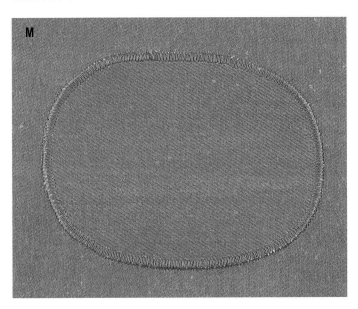

Mending a trouser pocket

Trouser pockets—or any pocket hanging inside a garment—can become worn, but can be easily fixed for a new lease on life.

1. Cut away the worn area and use it as a pattern. Cut a double layer of fabric using the pattern, adding on $\frac{3}{8}$ in. to the straight cut edges for seams.

2. Unpick the pocket seams a little way past the cut edges. Stitch the new pieces to the cut edges, taking $\frac{3}{8}$ in. for seams. Zigzag stitch the edges together and press downward.

3. Restitch the seam around the outer edge of the pocket and zigzag stitch the edges together (**N**).

Decorative patch

Sometimes, especially on children's clothes, it is possible to turn a repair into a decorative patch that is a feature as well as functional. An irregular shape and uneven stitching will add to the primitive charm. If the item is to be laundered frequently, the edge can be zigzag stitched before handstitching.

1. Apply fusible web to the wrong side of the patch fabric following the manufacturer's instructions. Cut out the patch to the required size and steam press to fuse the patch in place.

2. Handstitch large, uneven crossed stitches over the edges using a contrast embroidery thread (**O**).

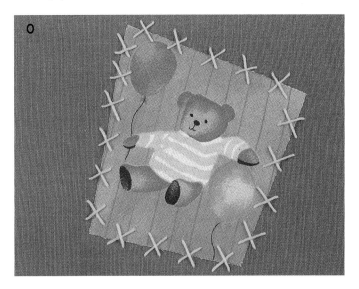

Calico Shopping Bag

This simple shopping bag is decorated with pretty appliqué daisies. You can use this method to add any design you like to a similar item.

MATERIALS
Pattern paper
$1\frac{1}{4}$ yd. print fabric
$1\frac{1}{4}$ yd. iron-on interfacing
$1\frac{1}{4}$ yd. lining fabric
$\frac{5}{8}$ yd. fusible web
Fabric scraps for appliqué

CUTTING OUT

1 Cut out a paper pattern $18\frac{1}{2}$ in. wide x $14\frac{1}{4}$ in. deep (includes $\frac{5}{8}$-in. seam allowances). Using the pattern, cut two pieces each from the print, interfacing, and lining. Cut two handles $3\frac{1}{2}$ x $23\frac{1}{2}$ in. from the print fabric.

2 Mark an area on your paper pattern $2\frac{1}{4}$ in. in from the side and base edges and $\frac{5}{8}$ in. down from the top edge of your front piece. Trace the flower design from page 92 and transfer it to the pattern (**diagram 1**), keeping within the marked area. You may need to scale the design up or down to fit.

STITCHING

1 Apply the iron-on interfacing to the wrong side of the print pieces. Lightly mark the positions for the flower stems on the front area on one print piece. Adjust the machine to a wide, close zigzag stitch and stitch the stems in satin stitch. Pull the thread end through to the wrong side and knot together to finish. Cut out and apply the appliqué design, stitching around the edges with a zigzag stitch.

2 Stitch the two print pieces facing together around the side and bottom edges. Stitch the linings together in the same way, but leave a 6 in. opening on the bottom edge. Press the seams open.

3 Open out the lower corners and refold them diagonally so the side and bottom seams are on top of the other at the center of the point. Stitch across at right angles to the seams $1\frac{1}{2}$ in. in from the point in the same way as for the zip-up bag. (See page 64.) Trim the point away above the stitching. Stitch the lining corners in the same way.

DIAGRAM 1

4 Press ⅝ in. to the wrong side along both long edges of the handles. Press the handles in half lengthwise and stitch along both long edges. With the handles pointing downward, pin and tack their ends to the top edge of the bag 4¼ in. from the side seams **(diagram 2)**.

DIAGRAM 2

5 Place the lining to the bag with right sides together and the top edges even so the handles are sandwiched, and stitch the lining to the bag around the top edge. Turn the bag right side out through the opening in the lining stitching. Handstitch the opening in the lining to close. Press the lining to the inside of the bag and topstitch around the top edge to finish.

MAKING A FIRM BASE

A fabric-covered cardboard insert will give the bag a firm base and help it keep its shape. First, cut the cardboard to the size of the bottom of the bag, then cut a piece of lining fabric twice as wide as the card, plus seam allowances all around. Fold the fabric in half, lengthwise, and stitch together along one short and one long edge. Turn the fabric right-side out and press. Slip the cardboard into the fabric sleeve, tuck in the remaining raw edges, and handstitch them together.

Wall Hanging with Pockets

Pockets of bold, bright colors add a modern look to this useful wall organizer. The spacious pockets have folded side gussets for extra space, making them great for storing toys, accessories, shoes—even your sewing kit! We used a different color fabric for each pocket, but this wall hanging would look just as good using the same color fabric for all of the pockets.

MATERIALS

2 yds. fabric (for background of hanging)

$\frac{1}{3}$ yd. each of 9 assorted cotton fabrics

$\frac{2}{3}$ yd. lining

CUTTING OUT

1 Cut two pieces of calico and one from the interlining, each 19 x $26\frac{3}{4}$ in. ($\frac{5}{8}$-in. seam allowances included). Cut a calico strip $4\frac{3}{4}$ x $31\frac{1}{2}$ in. for the tabs. Cut nine pockets from the fabric assortment, each 9 x $8\frac{1}{4}$ in.

STITCHING

1 Press $\frac{5}{8}$ in. to the wrong side down the two shorter side edges and the lower edge of the first pocket. Press a $\frac{3}{8}$ in., then a $\frac{3}{4}$ in. hem to the wrong side along the top edge and stitch in place. On each side edge, press $1\frac{1}{2}$ in. to wrong side, then $\frac{3}{4}$ in. back to the right side to form a gusset (**diagram 1**). Make up all nine pockets in this way.

DIAGRAM 1

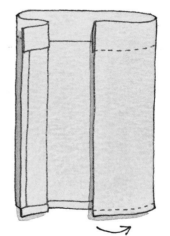

2 Arrange the pockets with the gussets folded in on one main piece of the backing fabric with the top edges of the top pockets about $2\frac{1}{2}$ in. down. Place the sides of the pockets about $\frac{3}{4}$ in. apart and allow $1\frac{1}{2}$ in. between the rows and at the side and bottom edges.

3 Pin the side edges of the pockets in place carefully, lifting up the gusset to do so. Stitch the two side edges of each pocket. Refold the gussets and stitch across the bottom edges with the gussets folded.

4 Fold the tab strip in half lengthwise and stitch along the length. Trim the seam, turn the tab right-side out, and press the seam at one edge. Topstitch the two long sides, near the edges .

5 Cut the tab strip into four equal lengths and fold each tab in half. Pin and tack the tabs in position, making sure that they are 1 in. from the side edges and evenly spaced. The tabs should point downward and the raw edges should be even (**diagram 2**).

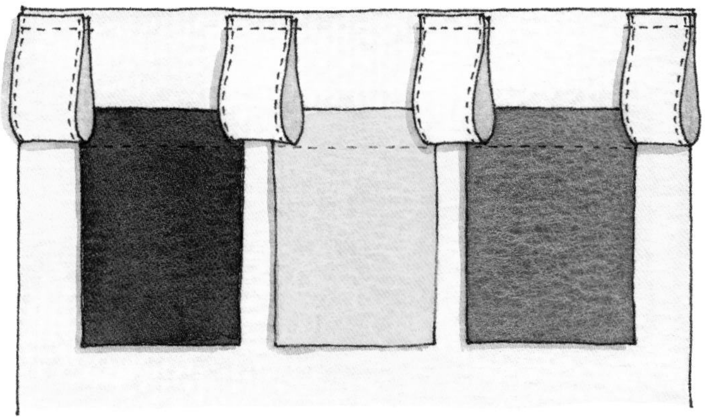

6 Place the lining to the wrong side of the backing piece, then place the remaining fabric piece to the right side of the backing. Stitch together through all layers leaving an 8 in. gap at the lower edge to turn through. Trim the lining from the seam allowance and trim the seam allowance and corners.

7 Turn the wall hanging right-side out and press the seam to the edge. Tuck in the seam allowances along the opening and handstitch the edges together. Topstitch around the outer edge of the wall hanging to finish if you like.

DIAGRAM 2

Silverware Roll

Add a refined touch to alfresco dining with an individual roll that keeps utensils in a divided pocket and unrolls to form a place-mat. Here, a toile de jouy fabric design with idyllic rural scenes perfectly echoes this outdoor theme.

MATERIALS
1$\frac{1}{4}$ yd. cotton toile de jouy fabric
$\frac{5}{8}$ yd. medium-weight interfacing
1$\frac{1}{4}$ yd. ribbon

CUTTING OUT

1 Cut out two fabric pieces and one interfacing piece, each 17$\frac{1}{4}$ x12 in. ($\frac{5}{8}$-in. seam allowances included), and a pocket 4$\frac{3}{4}$ x 7 in.

2 Cut a 1$\frac{3}{4}$ in.-wide bias strip long enough to fit around the outer edge of the finished roll, joining if required.

STITCHING

1 Sandwich the interfacing between the two fabric pieces with the fabric right sides out, and pin together. Using a small cup or jar as a template, draw around at the corners to make curved corners. Trim away the excess fabric. Baste together through all layers around the edge about $\frac{1}{4}$ in. in from the edge.

2 Press $\frac{5}{8}$ in. to the wrong side down the side edges of the pocket. Press $\frac{3}{8}$ in., then a $\frac{3}{4}$ in. hem to the wrong side across the top edge of the pocket and stitch in place.

3 Place the pocket on the mat with its side edge 1¼ in. from the side edge of the mat and its lower raw edge even with edge of the mat. Stitch in place down both side edges.

4 Stitch two more rows down the pocket, each 1¼ in. from the sides, to divide the pocket into three 1¼-in.-wide sections.

5 Fold the ribbon in half and tack the fold. On the opposite side edge to the pocket, tack the ribbon even with the edge of the mat at the center and on the other side of the mat (**diagram 1**).

6 Press the long edges of the crosswise strip toward the center of the strip so they nearly meet at the center, then press the strip in half so the bottom half is just slightly wider than the top half.

7 Arranging so the join will be on a straight edge, insert the edge of the mat inside the binding with the narrower half uppermost. Pin the binding in place, gently easing it, and steam press it to shape around the corners (**diagram 2**). Join the ends with a diagonal seam or by the overlapping method. (See page 35.) Machine-stitch the binding in place through all layers so that the fold of the ribbon is caught in the stitching.

DIAGRAM 1

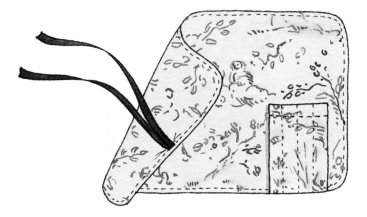

DIAGRAM 2

Calico Shopping Bag Template (See page 80.)

Suppliers

UNITED STATES

ABC Embroidered Accessories
1320 Boxwood Ave.
Gilbert, AZ 85233
(480) 545-0777
www.abclace.com

American & Efird
P.O. Box 507
Mt. Holly, NC 28120
(800) 847-3235
www.amefird.com

Bernina of America
www.berninausa.com

Brewer Sewing Supplies
3800 W. 42nd St.
Chicago, IL 60632
(800) 444-3111
www.brewersewing.com

Brother International
100 Somerset Corporate Blvd.
Bridgewater, NJ 08807
(908) 252-3042
www.brewersews.com

Butterick
www.mccall.com

C-Thru Ruler Co.
6 Britton Dr.
Bloomfield, CT 06002
(800) 243-8419
www.cthruruler.com

Coats & Clark
3430 Toringdon, Ste. 301
Charlotte, NC 28277
(704) 329-5009
www.coatsandclark.com

Dantex Trimmings & Textile Co.
270 W. 39th St.
New York, NY 10018
(212) 719-9640
www.dantextrimming.com

Dill Buttons of America
50 Choate Cir.
Montoursville, PA 17754
(888) 460-7555

Fabri-Quilt
9901 E. 14th Ave.
N. Kansas City, MO 64116
(816) 421-2000
www.fabri-quilt.com

Fiskars
7811 W. Stewart Ave.
Wausau, WI 54401
(800) 500-4849
www.fiskars.com

Gutermann of America
www.gutermann-us.com

Havel's
3726 Lonsdale St.
Cincinnati, OH 45227
(800) 638-4770
www.havels.com

HTCW
393 Crescent Ave,
Wyckoff, NJ 07841
(800) 275-4275
www.htcproducts.com

Husqvarnaviking
www.husqvarnaviking.com

McCall Pattern Co
www.mccall.com

Prym-Dritz
www.prym-dritz.com

Rhode Island Textile Co.
211 Columbus Ave.
Pawtucket, RI 02861

Simplicity
www.simplicity.com

Spectrix Fabrics
1359 Broadway, Ste. 1504
New York, NY 10018
(212) 629-8320
www.fabrics byspectrix.com

St. Louis Trimming, div. Of Trimtex
713 Barham Down Dr.
Ballwin, MO 63011
(636) 527-5552
www.stlouistrim.com

Sulky of America
3113 Broadpoint Dr.
Punta Gorda, FL 33983
(941) 629-3199
www.sulky.com

ASSOCIATIONS

American Craft Council
21 S. Eltings Corner Rd.
Highland, NY 12528
(800) 836-3470
www.craftcouncil.org

American Sewing Guild
9660 Hillcroft
Houston, TX 77096
(713) 729-3000
www.asg.com

Home Sewing Association
P.O. Box 1312
Monroeville, PA 15146
(412) 372-5950
www.sewing.org

Arts and Crafts Association of America
4888 Cannon Woods Ct.
Belmont, MI 49306
(616) 874-1721
www.artsandcraftsassoc.com

Association of Crafts & Creative Industries
1100-H Brandywine Blvd.
P.O. Box 3388
Zanesville, OH 43702
(740) 452-4541
www.accicrafts.org

Hobby Industry Association
319 E. 54th St.
Elmwood Park, NJ 07407
(201) 794-1133
www.hobby.org

National Craft Association
1945 E. Ridge Rd., Suite 5178
Rochester, NY 14622
(800) 715-9594

CANADA

Bernat
320 Livingstone Ave. S.
Listowel, ON N4W, CA
(591) 291-3780
www.bernat.com

Canada Craft and Hobby Association
#24 1410-40 Ave., N.E.
Calgary, AL T2E 6L1
(403) 291-0559

Canadian Crafts Federation c/o Ontario Crafts Council
Designers Walk
170 Bedford Rd., Suite 300
Toronto, ON M5R 2K9
(416) 408-2294
www.Canadiancraftsfederation.ca

Index

A

alterations
    curtains 28
    hems 24–25
appliqué 8, 75
aprons
    Child's Apron 30–32
    repairing a tear in 33

B

backstitch 13
bags
    Calico Shopping Bag 80–83
    Clothespin Bag 36–39
    Drawstring Bag 42–43
    Zip-Up Bags 62–65
basic information 8–11
bias
    cutting bias strips 66
    finding the 12
bias binding 35
blanket stitch 75
blind hen stitch 9
bold thread (buttonhole twist) 11
bows 74
braid 74
Buttoned Pillow 59–60
buttonhole stitch 9
buttonholes 8, 11, 56–57
buttons 55–56
    fabric-covered 56
    making a shank for a flat button 56
    moving 61
    stitching on a shank button 56
    stitching on flat buttons 55
    torn 61

C

calico 10
Calico Shopping Bag 80–83
cambric 10
casings 40–41
chain stitch 75
Chair-Seat Cover 70–71
    Pretty Paisley Chair-Seat Cover
        Variation 73
challis 10
chambray 10
Child's Apron 30–32
chintz 10
clothespin bag 36-39
cord stitching 74
corners
    attaching piping to 67
    mitering a corner 44

    stitching around 14
    trimming 17
cotton 9–10, 11
cotton thread 11
curtains 9, 10
    alterations 28
    Tie-top Curtains 26–28
curves
    attaching piping to 67
    stitching around 14
cutting out, tips for 80

D

denim 10
Diagonal Seam Pillow 20–21
Drawstring Bag 42–43
dressmaker's chalk 8, 9
dressmaker's pins 8, 9
dressmaker's shears 8, 9, 12
drill 10

E

edgestitching 17

F

fabric marker pen 8, 9, 12
fabrics
    and fullness 26
    calico 10
    cambric 10
    challis 10
    chambray 10
    chintz 10
    choosing 9–10
    cotton 9–10, 11
    cutting 12
    denim 10
    drill 10
    gingham 10
    joining 12
    lawn 10
    linen 10, 11
    man-made 10
    matching patterned 14–15
    nylon 10
    polyester 10
    polyester cotton voile 10
    poplin 10
    rayon 10
    silk 10, 11
    silk dupion 10
    silk organza 10
    ticking 10
    tweed 10
    voile 10

    wool 10, 11
fastenings 54–58
    buttons 55–56
    hooks and bars 58
    hooks and eyes 58
    nonsew stud 58
    press studs 58
    Velcro (TM) 58
    zippers 54–55, 64
    finishing touches 74–75
fly stitch 75

G

gathers 68
getting started 12–17
gingham 10

H

hems 22–25
    alterations 24–25
    basic 22
    curved 25
    double 22
    double-mitered 44
    hemstitched 23
    herringbone stitch hem 23
    machine-rolled 24
hemstitching
    hemstitched hem 23
    hemstitched fringe 74
hooks and bars 58
hooks and eyes 58

I

ironing board 8

L

lace 74
ladder stitch 13
lawn 10
linen 10, 11

M

machine-stitching 14–17
man-made fabrics 10
matching
    patterned fabrics 14
    seams 15
    stripes 15
mending
    a torn pocket 77
    a trouser pocket 79
    repairing a tear in an apron 33
mitered corners and borders 44–45

N
needles 8, 9
choosing 11
sewing machine 11
nylon 10

P
patches 78–79
decorative 79
handstitched 78
patch pockets 76
zig-zag stitched 78
pattern paper 80
pillows
Buttoned Pillow 59–60
Diagonal Seam Pillow 20–21
Striped Pillow Covers 18–20
pinking 17
pinning 12
pins 8, 9, 11
piping 66–67
pleats 69
pockets 76
divided 77
mending a torn pocket 77
Wall Hanging with Pockets 84–87
with gussets 76
polyester 10
polyester cotton voile 10
polyester thread 11
poplin 10
press studs 58

R
rayon 10
reverse stitching 14
right-angle set square 8, 9, 12
ruler 8, 9, 12
running stitch

S
satin stitch 8
scallops 34
scissors 8, 9
seams
curved 34
flat fell or shirt 16
French 16
layering 15
machine-stitched 15
matching 15
neatening 17
plain seam 15
snipping into 34
selvedges 12
sewing kit, basic 8
sewing machines 8, 9
needles 11
silk 10
silk dupion 10
silk organza 10
silk thread 11
Silverware Roll 88–91
Small cosmetic purse 62, 65
starting and finishing 13
steam iron 8, 9
stitches
backstitch 13
blanket stitch 75
blind hem 9
buttonhole 9
chain stitch 75
embroidery 75
fly stitch 75
ladder stitch 13
running stitch 13
satin stitch 8
straight 8
three-step zigzag (tricot) 8–9
zigzag 8
straight stitch 8
Striped Pillow Covers 18–20

T
Table Runner with Mitered Border
50–52
Table Runner with Two Borders 53
Tablecloth and Napkin 46–49
tablecloths
Table Runner with Mitered Border
50–52
Table Runner with Two Borders 53
Tablecloth and Napkin 46–49
tacking 12
tacking thread 11, 12
tape measure 8, 9
techniques 12–17
threads
bold thread (buttonhole twist) 11
choosing 10–11
cotton 11
polyester thread 11
silk 11
tacking 11, 12
three-step zigzag (tricot) stitch 8–9
ticking 10
ties 74
Tie-top Curtains 26–28
topstitching 34
trouser cuffs, shortening 23
trousers
mending a trouser pocket 79
shortening trouser cuffs 23
tweed 10

V
Velcro (TM) 58
voile 10
Wall Hanging with Pockets 84–87
wool 10, 11

Z
zigzag stitch 8, 17, 75
zippers 54–55
replacing a zipper 64
Zip-Up Bags 62–65